The U.S. Navy
and Marine Corps
Into the 21st Century

Photography by
Brian R. Wolff

Text by
John Alexander
Commander USN, Ret.

STACKPOLE
BOOKS

ISBN 1-85532-671-X

This edition published in the United States by
Stackpole Books, 5067 Ritter Road, Mechanicsburg, PA 17055

For a catalog of all books published by Osprey Military please write to:
Osprey Marketing, Reed Books, Michelin House, 81 Fulham Road, London,
England, SW3 6RB
Phone 171-225-9860 • Fax 171-225-9869

Book design by Studio 31, Inc.

Editor Shaun Barrington

Artwork on pages 240–241 copyright © John Batchelor

Printed in China

PAGE 1: *Sailors have been going to sea for centuries, but long separations and
saying goodbye don't get any easier with practice.*

TITLE PAGE: *This international carrier battle group is comprised of ships from
the United States and Australia which were participating in Exercise Tandem
Thrust '97. This Combined Joint Task Force exercise involved nearly four dozen
ships, and more than 27,000 service men and women. It was designed to
strengthen the alliance between the two countries to pursue common regional
and international security objectives and to contribute to the preservation
of security and strategic stability in the region.*

*In the early 1990s the Navy and Marine Corps expanded and refined their
strategic concept which they articulated in a planning document called "From
the Sea." We chose this title,* From the Sea *for our book because it explicitly
links the Naval Services' forward presence peacetime operations to its expeditionary, "joint" multi-service missions. The inherent value of the Navy-Marine
Corps Team is its unique visible presence, combat capabilities and ability to
respond rapidly to global threats, reacting before they escalate into crises. Our
forces can go anywhere, or almost anywhere without having to seek permission,
perform our mission as required, then return home.*

FRONT COVER: *The Aegis destroyer USS COLE fires a salvo of three Standard
SM-2 surface to air missiles during an exercise in the Caribbean Sea. The ships
of this class are among the most capable surface combatants in the world.*

Contents

STRATEGIC VISION BY SECRETARY OF THE NAVY JOHN H. DALTON 7

A MESSAGE FROM ADMIRAL JAY L. JOHNSON, USN
AND GENERAL CHARLES C. KRULAK, USMC 12

ACKNOWLEDGEMENTS 16

INTRODUCTION BY DR. COLIN GRAY 20

SURFACE COMBATANTS: BACKBONE OF THE FLEET 24

NAVAL AVIATION: WINGS OF GOLD 86

SUBMARINES: THE SILENT WORKHORSES 126

AMPHIBIOUS OPERATIONS: THE VALUE OF TEAMWORK 156

TRAINING: THE KEY TO READINESS 226

TECHNICAL APPENDICES 240

ABOVE: *The guided missile frigate USS ELROD (FFG-55) fires a missile in the Caribbean from its forward-mounted Standard Missile Launcher.*

Strategic Vision

by John H. Dalton, Secretary of the Navy

The Navy-Marine Corps Team navigates a course based on our continued emphasis on forward presence. It is a proven operating strategy, one that is remarkably responsive to changing threat and fiscal environments. Furthermore, our forward presence operations in peacetime drive the planning and preparation for the next conflict. Let me re-emphasize the major tenet of that strategic vision: Naval Expeditionary Forces — forward deployed — are the central element in meeting the national security objectives of the United States for the foreseeable future.

"Expeditionary" implies a mind set, a culture, and a commitment to fully integrated Marine and Navy forces that are designed to operate forward and to respond swiftly. They are structured to project power from the sea when required by National Command Authority. Perhaps most importantly, Naval Expeditionary Forces are largely unrestricted by the need for transit or overflight approval from foreign governments in order to enter the scene of action. We do not need anyone else's permission to get our job done. This is a unique attribute of the Sea Services, and it is one which will bear heavily on the future. Forward-deployed expeditionary operations are the basis of the *From the Sea* and the subsequent white paper, *Forward . . . From the Sea* which I signed with the Chief of Naval Operations and the Commandant of the Marine Corps. To summarize these papers in a single sentence, our strategy has shifted from focusing on a single global threat to regional challenges.

Bosnia is a good example. Look at the success of the Peace Talks in Dayton and the deployment of Allied Forces into Croatia and Bosnia. American military leadership — with the impressive use of airpower by the USS THEODORE ROOSEVELT and the USS AMERICA, and Tomahawk strikes by the USS NORMANDY — brought the warring factions to the table. Now the TR is back in the Mediterranean — soon to be replaced by the USS JOHN F. KENNEDY — keeping that hard-won peace.

But that is just one example. Events in Iraq this past fall are another case in point. Navy forces were on scene to deliver a very powerful message to Saddam Hussein. And our men and women are still there — on station, in the Gulf, launching aircraft to enforce the No-Fly Zone, and standing-by to launch more Tomahawk cruise missiles or precision air strikes. Remember the tensions in the Taiwan Strait in March 1996, or the evacuation of western business and government officials from Albania earlier this spring, or go back a bit further to Liberia, Rwanda, Somalia and Haiti? It is Navy and Marine Corps forces doing what they do best from

OPPOSITE: *In the Tactical Flag Command Center (TFCC) on board the USS CARL VINSON (CVN-72), an officer uses the Joint Primary Aircraft Training System (JPATS) to monitor air traffic.*

ABOVE: *Secretary Dalton at the christening of the Navy's newest nuclear-powered aircraft carrier, HARRY S. TRUMAN, on September 7, 1996 at Newport News, Virginia.*

"A" to "Z" — from Albania to Zaire, in peacetime, in war, and everything in between. America is getting a very solid return on its investment in these forward-deployed, forward-operating forces. Let me offer a few thoughts on this relationship between forward-deployed naval forces and political and economic stability.

A significant part of the mission of the Navy and Marine Corps is promoting and protecting our business interests — and that means protecting American jobs. The nation's wealth depends on attractive returns on investments in the United States and abroad. And, clearly, sound investment opportunities are created in secure, stable environments. But the reverse is also true.

The Gulf War is the most recent example of the consequences of instability. In addition to the human rights and international behavior issues associated with a foreign invasion, the following figures demonstrate the global impact of modern war: when the Iraqis invaded Kuwait, oil prices more than doubled overnight — from $19 per barrel to $42. In the first year after the invasion, it is estimated that the U.S. economy lost $60 billion in exports and $200 billion in lost productivity. That figure world-wide was about $1 trillion!

The Taiwan election crisis last year is a second example to illustrate the relationship between maritime presence and economic stability. As tensions between Taiwan and China escalated in the run-up to the elections, stock prices plunged in both Hong Kong and Taiwan. These markets recovered sharply after President Clinton announced the deployment of the USS INDEPENDENCE and the USS NIMITZ battlegroups toward the Taiwan Strait.

When I visited the Asia-Pacific in the spring of 1996, Australian Prime Minister John Howard, and the Singaporean Foreign Minister both thanked me personally — and asked me to thank President Clinton — for this demonstration of forward presence. Clearly our friends in the region credited our timely response for the region's secure economic and political environment. The bottom line is that the U.S. military, and in particular the Navy's forward-deployed forces, remain contributors to political stability and an agreeable business climate abroad, which in turn have provided a generally healthy economy at home.

If global stability is a vital national objective, then it is obvious that the U.S. and our allies must maintain — even in a world that contains just one superpower — a level of military security that can operate forward whether to support humanitarian operations, to keep the peace . . . or to make peace whenever and wherever required. Right now, more than half of our Navy is underway; 35% — or 122 ships — are forward deployed for six months. We have aircraft carrier battlegroups and amphibious ready groups operating in the Mediterranean and the Arabian Gulf, and along the southwest coast of Africa and the Pacific Rim. The forward presence of these forces is vital, but not always as visible to Americans as it is to the rest of the world. Yet, forward-deployed U.S. forces — primarily naval expeditionary forces — are crucial to regional stability. The United States must maintain the degree of vigilance necessary to ensure a secure global economic climate.

Regional instability is a constant in our world. Looking across history, the Cold War was an anomaly. It is not likely that we will ever live again in a bipolar world whose nuclear shadow suppressed nationalism and ethnic tensions. We have, in some respects, reverted back to the world familiar to our forefathers. Albania, Bosnia, Liberia, Iraq, Zaire, and the Taiwan Strait are merely examples of the types of continuing crises we will face tomorrow and 20 years from now.

Our strategic vision must be driven by selective and committed engagement, unilateral global operations, and prompt crisis resolution. This is the basis of our National Security Strategy. And, there is no better way to maintain and enforce these concepts than with the forward presence of the Navy-Marine Corps Team. As Chief of Naval Operations Admiral Jay Johnson, Marine Corps Commandant General Charles Krulak, and I see it, there are four basic tenets to international security in today's world: prevention, deterrence, crisis resolution and war termination. The underlying assumption of these tenets is that the United States and its allies should not be forced into winning a war in an overwhelming and expensive manner. Instead, it is much better and cheaper to resolve a crisis before it gets out of control. This is where the Sea Services earn their pay.

The first tenet is prevention — or preventing crises before they occur. The key to prevention is our presence in a region. Having Naval Expeditionary Forces on the scene lets our friends know we have an interest and lets potential foes know that we are there to check any move — and we need not take any direct action.

The second area is deterrence. Presence does not prevent every crisis. Some rogue states or groups will be tempted to strike no matter what the odds and will require active measures to be deterred. When crises reach this threshold, there is no substitute for sustained presence on the scene. Friends and potential enemies both recognize naval forces as capable of defending or destroying. It may be hard to quantify the cost savings of deterring a crisis before it requires our intervention. But the savings are real in dollars and often in blood and human misery.

Crisis resolution is the third tenet. If we cannot prevent or deter a crisis, then we must respond with prompt and decisive action to resolve the situation. Perhaps most important, naval expeditionary forces do not need permission from foreign governments to be on the scene and to take unilateral action in a crisis. This both frees the force to respond to national tasking and takes the pressure off allies to host any outside forces.

The fourth tenet of our national security strategy is conflict termination, or what some call "securing the peace." Each of the above tenets is worthy of the United States paying an annual peace insurance premium. Otherwise, we and our allies risk paying the emotional, physical and financial costs of a full-blown conflagration that began as just another brush fire. If there is a war, naval expeditionary forces will be first to fight. They are capable of enabling the follow-on forces from the United States for as long as it takes. And they will remain on-scene to enforce settlement that ends the conflict.

These basic elements of our national security strategy — prevention, deterrence, crisis resolution and war termination — demand a ready, capable and flexible force. This force must be prepared for the Iraqs, Central Africas, Somalias and Bosnias that inevitably destabilize and erode world order and respect for the rule of law. Indeed, a failure to respond to them encourages future, more serious crises. For the United States, maintaining a steady commitment to stability will be a challenge. But maintain it we must, or the price, literally and figuratively, will be much greater down the road. As we see demonstrated time and again — and I do not expect any changes for the foreseeable future — all of this is happening now forward, and most of it is happening from the sea. As the United States continues to withdraw from overseas bases, Naval Forces will become even more important in meeting American forward presence requirements. The bottom line is that we must maintain maritime forces forward to balance that loss of permanent presence.

I would like you to remember this. The Navy and Marine Corps are forward-looking, forward-operating forces. We are on station right now, ready to answer all bells. Our Sailors and Marines are trained and capable professionals. That is something for which I am tremendously grateful. And, it is something that all of America can look on with a great deal of pride. God bless you, and God bless America.

John H. Dalton

A Message
from Admiral Jay L. Johnson
and General Charles C. Krulak

This morning, as is the case every morning, keys are turning in the front doors of thousands of American business offices "forward deployed" literally all over the world. American companies invest in overseas presence because actually "being there" is clearly the best way to do business.

Also this morning, United States Navy amphibious assault ships carrying 4,400 combat-ready American Marines are forward deployed in the waters of the Mediterranean Sea and the Persian Gulf. And at sea in the Mediterranean and in the Persian Gulf are aircraft carrier battle groups with 16,000 Sailors and two airwings of combat-ready aircraft. Finally, in the Far East, the United States has permanently deployed a third aircraft carrier battle group and a third amphibious ready group. The vigilant "forward presence" of these forces is vital, but not always visible to Americans as it is to the rest of the world. Their routine, daily efforts don't always make the headlines . . . but they are vitally important to world peace and stability.

We have witnessed the end of the Cold War. Never again will we live in a bipolar world whose nuclear shadow suppressed nationalism and ethnic tensions. We have, in some respects, reverted back to the world our ancestors knew, a world in disorder. Somalia, Bosnia, Liberia, Haiti, Rwanda, Iraq, and the Taiwan Straits are merely examples of the "brushfire-type" crises we have and will continue to face. Some might call this period an age of chaos. As a key player in the world arena, the United States is often called upon to maintain international stability, preventing a specific crisis from escalating into threats to the United States', and the world's, vital interests. And while the skies are not dark with smoke from the brush-

fires, today's world demands a new approach. The concepts of choice must be selective and committed engagement, unencumbered global operations and prompt crisis resolution. There is no better way to maintain and enforce these concepts than with the forward presence of the U. S. Navy-Marine Corps Team.

It is forward deployed U.S. forces, primarily naval expeditionary forces — the Navy-Marine Corps Team — that are vital to regional stability and to keeping these crises

PRECEDING PAGES: *Lieutenant John "OB" O'Brien is an F-14 Tomcat pilot assigned to VF-154, deployed on board the USS INDEPENDENCE (CV-62).*

from escalating into full-scale wars. To those who contend that the United States can't afford to have this degree of vigilance any more, we say: "The United States can't afford not to."

Marines and Sailors embarked aboard Navy ships provide the National Command Authority (NCA) with a "rheostat" of national response capabilities. Naval expeditionary forces, like the ones pictured in this book, are self-contained air, land and sea strike force, operating from a protected sea base that can be tailored to meet any contingency. Whether deterring crises through presence, conducting disaster relief or humanitarian operations, the Navy-Marine Corps Team is globally engaged today and prepared for employment tomorrow. Moreover, employment of these flexible forces comes at little or no extra cost because these capabilities have already been bought and paid for! No other nation in the world possesses the politically and operationally flexible "rheostat" of national response capabilities offered by Marine forces aboard Navy ships.

The world's premier expeditionary force-in-readiness, the Navy-Marine Corps Team, is well positioned to lead the way into the 21st century. It is through the dedication, perseverance and professionalism of our Sailors and Marines that we are this Nation's force of choice, vanguards of the freedom we so gratefully enjoy. Sustained by a tradition of spirit of innovation and adaptability and the heart of the warrior, we will continue to be this Nation's force in readiness.

The United States must foster stability around the world . . . today, and tomorrow. The peace insurance premium is a small price and is the cost of leadership. Who else is capable of this type of forward presence on a global basis? For the United States, maintaining a steady commitment to stability will be a challenge. But maintain it we must, or the price, literally and figuratively, will be much greater down the road.

America's Navy-Marine Corps Team is underway, ready and on-scene at trouble spots around the world. Forward presence makes it — and will keep it — the right force, tailor-made for these uncertain and sometimes fiery times.

Jay L. Johnson
Admiral
United States Navy

Charles C. Krulak
General
United States Marine Corps

Photographer's Acknowledgments

In the early part of the 1980s when I was covering science and technology for *Science Digest* magazine, the editor told me that someone from the Navy had requested a meeting with me. That person was Tom Hall. I should have realized then that this was the beginning of a strange odyssey for a photojournalist living in New York. It was obvious that Tom Hall had been observing my stories and was briefed on how I worked. Ten minutes into the meeting he asked me if I would like to document the U.S. Navy. Without realizing how big the U.S. Navy was and not thinking of how long it would take. I dove into the project head first. It appeared I was enlisted: without

signing any papers, given rank or even a permanent bunk! My only pass was to be my camera, my only compensation from the Navy was having the opportunity to meet and photograph the wonderful professionals you will see in this book.

After Tom Hall recruited me for this project it was up to the people at CHINFO (Chief Of Information) to do all of the paperwork and help convince all of the people in the fleets to allow me entry into their lives. I grew for over 15 years with these people. I went through three Admirals at CHINFO who supported me and towards the end ADM Pease and his staff offered the critique and guidance to polish off this project. To all of the PAO's (Public Affairs Officers) at CHINFO who dealt with my many calls and lost as much sleep as I did over this project, I cannot thank you enough.

When I was traveling around the world my wife was home editing and syndicating the images to help raise the funds for the next trip, simultaneously

raising our son and creating a normal household. A task beyond my capabilities. Without Judy this book would have never happened. Thank you Judy and Stephen: without you two this book would be meaningless.

I hope you enjoy this brief look at some of the most incredibly professional people in the world and remember while traveling, if you get into some trouble in some foreign land, look out over the horizon and chances are that some Sailor or Marine will be coming to the rescue *From the Sea.*

THIS BOOK IS DEDICATED TO
EVERYONE WHO HAS SERVED OR IS SERVING
AS A MEMBER OF OUR ARMED FORCES.

YOU SERVE AS A ROLE MODEL BY YOUR SACRIFICE, INITIATIVE,
PERSEVERANCE AND COMMITMENT TO EXCELLENCE.

THANK YOU FOR PROTECTING OUR FREEDOM.

Author's Acknowledgments

I met Brian Wolff fifteen years ago while serving in New York City as a Navy Public Affairs Officer. He contributed to both of my earlier books. I wish to express my sincere appreciation to him for his confidence in making me a partner in this showcase of his photographic genius. His images tell such a wonderful story that attempting to enhance them with words proved a difficult task. Even more difficult was the job of reducing his inventory of more than a half-million color slides to the 300 photographs appearing in this book.

Saying "Thank you" seems insufficient to all of the individuals who shared their personal experiences by writing first-hand accounts in this volume. Their stories add authenticity that all of my research couldn't capture. I'm indebted to Secretary of the Navy John Dalton, Chief of Naval Operations Admiral Jay L. Johnson, Marine Corps Commandant General C.C. Krulak, and Dr. Colin Gray, renowned naval strategist, who collectively set the tone for this project and put it in proper perspective.

To Lieutenant Commander Hal Pittman, Captain Stephen Pietropaoli, and Rear Admiral Kendell Pease who effectively monitored our progress, kept us on course, opened otherwise closed doors, and jump-started the project when it occasionally stalled in the fleet, many, many thanks. Your assistance, and that of countless other Navy and Marine Corps public affairs officers, both active duty and civilian, who helped coordinate our efforts was invaluable to our success.

Finally, but far from least, I want to thank my wife of 25 years, Theresa, our son Richard, and our daughter Catherine, for their love, support and understanding. This project took me away from them on far too many weekends, and even when I was home, most of my time was spent on the computer.

PRECEDING PAGES: *The USS NORFOLK (SSN-714) cuts a wide wake as she prepares to leave her Norfolk, Virginia home port.*

OVERLEAF: *The Navy has the unique capability of inserting forces from any branch of our Armed Forces to almost anywhere in the world. Here, Army special forces commandos leap into the water from a CH-47 helicopter flown from the deck of an aircraft carrier.*

Introduction
by Dr. Colin Gray

Do you remember Humphrey Bogart as Commander Queeg, USN? The hero of Herman Wouk's brilliant novel, *The Caine Mutiny*, is the U.S. Navy, and the U.S. Navy, above all else, is people. Those people, the professionals of the U.S. sea services, stand between us civilians and some of the rougher realities of the world out there. With empathy, pathos, and irony, Wouk showed through fiction just how much America owes to its naval professionals. To understand, really to understand, what the U. S. Navy and Marine Corps do, and why it matters, don't read scholarly books on maritime strategy — at least don't read such books exclusively — read instead *The Caine Mutiny*. The Jewish defense counsel for the Caine "mutineers," Lt. Barney Greenwald, USN, explains drunkenly as follows, just why it is he is unhappy with the courtroom humiliation and defeat of Commander Queeg:

"See, while I was studying law 'n' old Keefer here was writing his play for the Theater Guild, and Willie here was on the playing fields of Princeton, all that time these birds we call regulars — these stuffy, stupid Prussians, in the Navy and the Army — were manning guns. 'Course they weren't doing it to save my mom from Hitler, they were doing it for dough, like everybody else does what they do. Question is, in the last analysis — last analysis —what do you do for dough? Old Yellowstain, [Commander Queeg] for dough, was standing guard on this fat, dumb and happy country of ours. Meantime me, I was advancing my little free non-Prussian life for dough. Of course, we figured in those days, only fools go into armed service. Bad pay, no millionaire future, and you can't call your mind or body your own. Not for sensitive intellectuals. So when all hell broke loose and the Germans started running out of soap and figured, well it's time to come over and melt down old Mrs. Greenwald — who's gonna stop them? Not her boy Barney. Can't stop a Nazi with a lawbook. So I dropped the lawbooks and ran to learn how to fly. Stout fellow. Meantime, and it took a year and a half before I was any good, who was keeping Mama out of the soap dish? Captain Queeg.

"Yes, even Queeg, poor sad guy, yes, and most of them not sad at all, fellows, a lot of them sharper boys than any of us, don't kid yourself, best men, I've ever seen, you can't be good in the Army or Navy unless you're goddamn good. Though maybe not up on Proust 'n' Finnegans Wake and all."

Powerful stuff — and true! As only a great novelist can, Wouk gets to the heart of the matter. We civilians can live our lives as we wish, make money and the rest, because somewhere "out there" professional guardians stand on watch for us.

A Navy cannot be bought or rented on a cost-effective, flexible, "as needed" basis. A Navy and Marine Corps are ready for war only because they have stayed sharp in time of peace. A great Navy cannot be created overnight, no matter how generous the Congress wishes to be. In fact, a great Navy cannot be created in a few years, possibly not even a few decades. British admirals have liked to boast, self-servingly, that it takes centuries to make a naval tradition. That is an exaggeration, but one that errs in the right direction. A great Navy is the product of decades of national investment in materiel and, most especially, in people. In addition, it is the living expression of what most aptly can be called a "tradition of victory."

In World War I, the Imperial German Navy, for all its technical achievement, lacked faith in itself. That Navy was half-defeated before it put to sea by its lack of tradition of any sort, let alone a "tradition of victory." Historians of the naval side of World War I advise us that the most critical advantage enjoyed by Britain's Royal Navy in that conflict was not its lead in numbers, most certainly was not in the realm of net technical superiority, but rather in what the leading American historian of the Royal Navy, Arthur J. Mader, called "the human factor." Mader concluded his massive (five volume) history of the Royal Navy, *In the Fisher Era, 1904-1919*, by advising that "the German Navy collapsed in part because it overlooked the fundamental truth that the human factor is always the "decisive one." He proceeded to note that, "basically . . . what ailed the German Navy was the absence of a maritime tradition."

The U.S. Navy is the modern heir to Britannia's trident. The story of the Royal Navy's moral superiority over the Imperial German Navy is important because it illustrates an enduring truth. In the days of "fighting sail," France and Spain both built handier warships than did Britain. But, because of the "human factor," in the Napoleonic Wars, the French set sail — on the rare occasions when it did — expecting to be defeated. To modernize this tale, even the most careful technical analyses of probable combat outcomes of East-West war at sea in the 1980s, could not really begin to capture the probable consequences of the confidence of the people in the U.S. Navy in themselves as a team with a long "tradition of victory" behind them. Of course, technology matters. But, always provided you are not on the wrong end of a catastrophic technological or other material shortfall, victory or defeat will be driven by the relative combat effectiveness of your people.

Contemporary strategic theory and defense analysis is apt to confuse bombardment with war and weapons with military effectiveness. Wonderful weapons will only ever be as wonderful in military effect as are the people who operate them, and as wonderful in ultimate strategic effect as is the quality of higher command and policy that they serve. It is necessary to advertise the vital importance of sea-service people, because so much of the publicly visible sea-service action appears as machines in motion. Some readers might believe, mistakenly, that my emphasis upon "the human factor" is just another example of current political correctness. Nothing could be further from the truth. The most relevant and persisting truth of strategic history is that although naval technology matters, the quality of Navy and Marine personnel matters more. Even had the Soviet Navy of the early 1980s not suffered from problems of (selective) technical disadvantage, unfortunate geography, and shortage of numbers in some key categories, still it would have lost in war at sea. The U.S. Navy had better people and benefited from the confidence that flows from a "tradition of victory."

As a strategic historian and theorist who is entirely alert and friendly to change in matters military, I continue to marvel at how little the strategic world really alters over long periods. At the beginning of the Twentieth Century some persuasive geopolitical theorists advised that whereas the four centuries from 1500 to 1900 had been a

"Columbian era" wherein "seapower ruled," this modern age, in contrast, would reward great continental empires with hegemony. Those theorists were both right and wrong, but mainly wrong! The Twentieth Century has not witnessed any eclipse of seapower at the hands of landpower (or even the new instruments of airpower, spacepower, now cyberpower). Rather, this century has seen maritime coalitions continue to triumph over continental coalitions — as they have throughout the course of modern history — but with the dominant seapower of those coalitions residing more and more plainly in the policy hands of a continental-size power, like the United States. The "owner" of dominant seapower has changed from 1900 to 2000, but the importance of seapower has not.

The fundamental reasons why the sea services are scarcely less significant today than they were a century ago are not exactly hard to find. In raw geographical terms, all, or nearly all, of the seas on earth are one. Geostrategically appraised, the seas, and the Navy that dominates those seas, unite the insular landmasses. Almost as much to the point is an assertion by Alfred Thayer Mahan that, incredibly perhaps, is almost as true today as when he first published it in 1890. The great man claimed that "notwithstanding all the familiar and unfamiliar dangers of the sea, both travel and traffic by water have always been easier and cheaper than by land." These days, for the United States, you can bombard from the air and through space, but if you need to transport heavy and very bulky goods over great distances, you can do so only by sea.

Over the past century, governments, publics, and certainly many strategic theorists, quite understandably, have been excited by the arrival of airpower, nuclear weapons, ballistic missiles and space systems, and — most recently — by the technologies for various kinds of information warfare. The excitement has waxed and then waned, leaving the practical duties, enabling functions, and general strategic effectiveness of the sea services very much as they were before. What has happened is that the United States Navy and Marine Corps have co-opted each new instrument — air, ballistic and cruise missile, space, and cyber — and used it to enhance their prowess and potency. The air, space, and "cyber" (or electromagnetic) environments have arrived as overlays upon the land and the sea, but they have not, and cannot, retire those traditional geographies as bases and foci for military activity.

Given the awesome technical changes registered in this century, it is perhaps amazing how little really has changed in the strategic functions of naval and amphibious power. Whether we focus upon the nature and workings of the Navy, or upon what the Navy contributes to national and international security, nothing essential has changed in a hundred years. Naval, and naval-relevant technologies have altered massively, but the importance of the person-machine interface, and especially of the quality of the people in question, has not altered.

More than 70 percent of the earth's surface is water; landmasses, greater or lesser, are nonetheless insular, and everything that flies has to pay heavy dues to the laws of physics. Geography and geophysics can be exploited by advancing technology, but they cannot be negated thereby. Provided it enjoys some forward logistic support in the form of a suitable fleet train or advanced base, the Navy can "loiter with latent menace" or "loiter to reassure" in ways thoroughly unavailable to the Army or Air Force. It is in the very nature of ships at sea — with tolerable forward base support — to be able to project U.S. power and influence in a manner that is flexibly visible, that can persist over time, yet which does not entangle with regional, political or geographical terrain.

For a world whose surface is mainly water, and for a country like the United States that is geostrategically effectively insular, and flanked by great oceans, the strategic case for superior maritime power all but makes itself. That superior U. S. maritime power is not really a competitor with airpower, spacepower, cyberpower, or whatever, rather is it the most critical enabling agent that provides leverage for U.S. military capabilities of all kinds. There is nothing on, or even plausibly over, the strategic horizon in the next century at all likely to retire the U.S. Navy and Marine Corps into the column of "yesterday's instruments." If seapower could claim the Twentieth Century as its own, as certainly it could for the Nineteenth, there should be scant reason to fear that the Twenty-First Century will reveal truly terminal challenges to this form of power.

The story of the Navy and Marine Corps over the past century therefore is one of both technical-tactical adaptation, and of strategic persistence. To understand strategically what the U. S. Sea Services contributed to the national security a century ago, is, with trivial need for modernization, to understand what they contribute today, and should contribute tomorrow. There has been a huge growth in the responsibilities of U.S. seapower, following, necessarily, the strategic demand generated by U.S. foreign policy. Thus far no evidence has appeared which would suggest that more is asked of the Navy and the Marine Corps than contemporary conditions allow them to perform.

By way of conclusion, I suggest humbly that the readers of this arresting book should approach the photographs as presenting contemporary shots of what amounts to an eternal story, really, perhaps, to the eternal story of the triangular relations among people, material artefacts, and raw geography — humans, ships (etc.), and the sea. Each image is immediate, it is "now," but also it is truly eternal.

Colin Gray

Dr. Colin Gray

Dr. Colin S. Gray is a political scientist with broad interests in national security policy, strategic theory and military history. Born in Oxfordshire, U.K. in 1943, Professor Gray moved to the U.S. in 1976 when he became Director of National Security Studies at the Hudson Institute, New York. He became an American citizen in 1981. From 1982 to 1987 he served on the President's General Advisory Committee on Arms Control and Disarmament. In April 1987 he was presented with the Superior Public Service Award by the U.S. Department of the Navy. He has served on advisory panels for the Congressional Office of Technology Assessment (SDI and space weapons), the Department of the Army (tactical nuclear weapons), the Department of the Air Force (innovations), and the U.S. Space Command (future of space forces). Among his many published books are *The Leverage of Sea Power – The Strategic Advantage of Navies in War* (1992); and *The Navy in the Post-Cold War World* (1994).

PREVIOUS PAGES: *Despite the rough seas, Sailors on board the destroyer the USS HAYLER (DD-997) man the lines during underway replenishment in the North Atlantic. A good test of seamanship skills, the two ships routinely steer a parallel course at 15 knots, maintaining a constant separation of just 100 feet.*

ABOVE AND OPPOSITE: *Knowing they'll be gone for six months or more, it is difficult to end the last kiss, embrace or goodbye wave. Often, family members, loved ones and friends will watch departing ships until they are out of sight.*

OVERLEAF: *The USS HAYLER steams through white caps in the North Atlantic. In the distance, the replenishment oiler the USS SAVANNAH (AOR-4) provides needed supplies to two ships simultaneously.*

Anyone who has suffered through a lengthy deployment knows what it means to "put on a happy face." Husbands and wives want to send their spouses off to sea in a happy frame of mind, so they attempt to reassure them that they will carry on just fine in their absence. But their bright smiles, shining eyes and enthusiastic arm-waving are sometimes unconvincing masks for the emotional turmoil associated with separation. There is a long-standing truism devoid of humor about car breakdowns, roofs that spring leaks, unexpected costly illnesses, children's truancy from school — the list of crises is endless — all occurring just after YOUR ship has sailed out of sight. Fortunately, the Sailors and Marines that form the Navy and Marine Corps Team are part of a large, close-knit family. They embody the motto, "The Navy & Marine Corps — We Take Care of Our Own!" And simply by joining the team, each new service spouse and each of their children has a support network without equal. Organizations including Wives' Clubs, Family Serivces Centers, and the Navy-Marine Corps Relief Society exist to respond to their emergency needs. And knowing that this safety net is in place allows members of our Navy-Marine Corps Team to focus on their job responsibilities and the mission at hand.

OPPOSITE: *First ship of the DDG-51 class, the USS ARLEIGH BURKE was commissioned on the Fourth of July, 1991. This class of ship was named after the legendary Admiral Arleigh Burke, the most famous destroyerman of World War II, and former Chief of Naval Operations. Admiral Burke died on New Year's Day, 1996. The signal flags read, "USS ARLEIGH BURKE DDG-51."*

ABOVE: *A signalman on board the USS ARLEIGH BURKE hoists signal flags. Despite sophisticated communications systems, signal flags are not susceptible to electronic interference or interception, and they remain an effective way for ships in the same vicinity to communicate important information to each other.*

The Legacy of Aegis

"Aegis is a legacy, a model, and a family. Anyone who has sailed in an Aegis cruiser or destroyer knows this. Anyone who hasn't, senses it. Most importantly, Aegis endures. It does so because it so readily adapts to the timeless demands of naval warfare. For all this, we should be thankful to our forefathers who had the vision and wisdom to design and introduce this magnificent shield to the fleet. These pictures have captured the fortunate inheritors of that legacy.

Legacies don't come easily. Many forces challenge their staying power. Those that survive indeed thrive on the challenge of enduring. The key is to continually contribute value to the Navy. Aegis does just that. Its

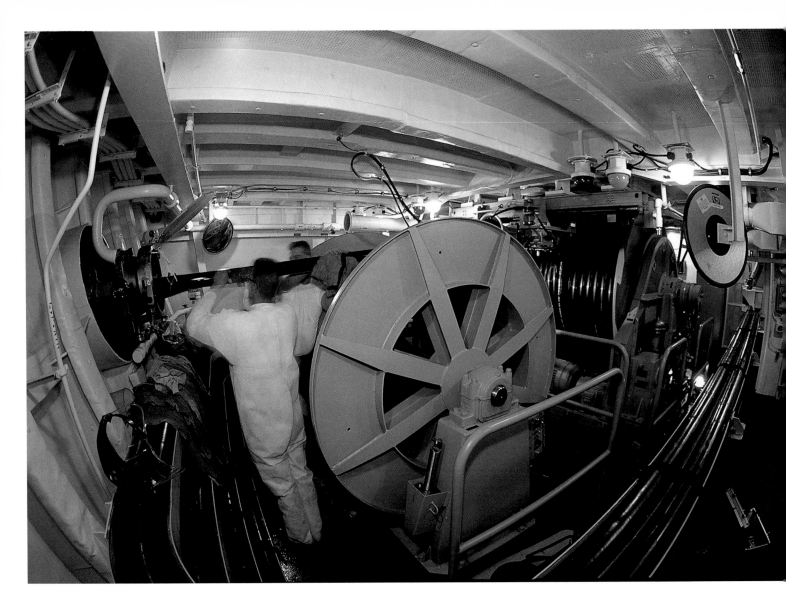

innovation and application are now being adopted by other navies around the world. Our Japanese and Spanish allies are building Aegis destroyers. More navies will follow because of the elegance of the Aegis solution. That's what legacies are made of.

The Aegis program has been a model for setting standards in ship-building. Build a little, test a little, build a little has been the Aegis mantra. Recognizing that continuous improvement is predicated on an incremental approach to making sure the next ship is better than its predecessor. I will always remember telling Captain Gary Roughead, the CO of DDG-52, that our primary goal in the ARLEIGH BURKE was to make sure that the second ship of the Aegis destroyer class was better than the first.

Finally, Aegis is a family. Perhaps that is the greatest accomplishment. This magnificent technology manifests itself in the hands of men and women who take these powerful ships to sea. Right behind them is a truly remarkable infrastructure of engineers, support teams, managers, and leaders. Shoulder to shoulder, it is this team of unrivaled Americans that make the Aegis family a legacy.

Admiral Burke's destroyer is 505 feet of American fighting steel. Legacy. Model. Family. It's the heart of our Navy."

— Captain John Morgan,
First Commanding Officer of the USS ARLEIGH BURKE

The Aegis system was designed as a total weapon system, from detection to kill. The heart of the system is an advanced, high-powered, automatic detect, track, multi-function phased-array radar capable of performing search, track and missile guidance functions on more than 100 targets simultaneously. The computer-based command and decision element is the core of the Aegis combat system.

This inter-face makes the Aegis combat system capable of simultaneous operation against a multi-mission threat: anti-air, anti-surface and anti-submarine warfare. The Navy built the first Aegis cruisers using the hull and machinery designs of Spruance-class destroyers.

The commissioning of the USS BUNKER HILL (CG-52) opened a new era in surface warfare as the first Aegis ship outfitted with the Vertical Launching System, which allows a more various missile selection, greater firepower and survivability.

OPPOSITE: *When in use, this towed array sonar equipment is trailed behind the ship at various depths to detect submarines.*

ABOVE: *Aegis destroyers like the USS ARLEIGH BURKE are positive pressure ships. Seen here is a special shower that any crew member who has been exposed to nuclear, biological or chemical warfare agents passes through to minimize risk of injury.*

ABOVE: *Ship movements continue despite cold weather and snow. As a Norfolk-based ship gets underway, a Sailor lowers the Union Jack which is flown from the jack staff on the bow of every U.S. Navy ship when in port.*

OPPOSITE, TOP: *Pallets of ammunition delivered from the Naval Weapons Station, Yorktown, must be inspected and inventoried before storage.*

OPPOSITE, BOTTOM: *Sailors on board the USS ARLEIGH BURKE (DDG-51) maneuver an acoustic homing torpedo with the ship's deck crane. The Arleigh Burke's combat system includes the Mark 41 Vertical Launching System (VLS), an advanced anti-submarine warfare system, advanced anti-air warfare missiles, and Tomahawk land-attack cruise missiles, in a potent, multi-mission (ASW, AAW, ASUW, and Strike) platform. This class of ships will also provide future Area and Theater-wide defense against ballistic and overland cruise missiles.*

BELOW : *No ship stands alone. At the Typhoon Warning Center on Guam, a watchstander monitors the weather around the world with a real-time satellite, and via data transmission, can warn ships standing into danger.*

OPPOSITE: *The USS ARLEIGH BURKE sails on top of the world and can receive information from the Typhoon Warning Center via the small antenna located to the right of the domed radar.*

OVERLEAF: *A battleship fires her massive 16-inch guns. After Desert Storm, the World War II-vintage battlewagons were returned to mothballs. Despite being manpower intensive and costly to maintain, the Marines revered battleships for their shore bombardment and gunfire support capabilities.*

PAGES 40–41: *The guided missile destroyer the USS DAHLGREN (DDG-43) underway beneath gray skies in the North Atlantic with the frigate the USS ROBERT G. BRADLEY (FFG-49) in the distance; the American flag provides the only color.*

Mines: Ever-present Hazard

On April 15, 1988, the frigate USS SAMUEL B. ROBERTS struck a mine in the Persian Gulf. The mine temporarily crippled the ship, but not the men onboard. In the face of adversity, the ship's commanding officer, Captain Paul Rinn, summed it up best in talking with a Navy television crew who happened to be aboard the ROBERTS when the ship struck the mine:

"The story that has unfolded here over the last 30 hours is the story of a ship that refused to die — of a crew that is well trained and well disciplined; that has tremendous pride and tremendous spirit. Such ordeals strengthen the fiber binding our Navy family together. I'm very proud of the men aboard this ship, and they are very proud of themselves and their Navy."

— Captain Paul Rinn, U.S. Navy
Now serving as Special Assistant to the Chief of Naval Operations

These pages show an underway replenishment, or UNREP, in the North Atlantic. By deploying supply ships with fuel, food, ammunition, spare parts and other cargo, the Navy can conduct sustained operations at sea without having to come into port.

OVERLEAF: *Much of the underway replenishment is provided by units of the Military Sealift Command's Naval Fleet Auxiliary Force like USNS WACCAMAW, at right, sending a fuel hose to the guided missile destroyer USS RICHARD E. BYRD in the North Atlantic. The primary mission of the Military Sealift Command is to provide sea transportation of equipment, supplies and ammunition to sustain U.S. forces worldwide during peacetime and in war for as long as operational requirements dictate. The Persian Gulf war underscored once again the vital role of the Military Sealift Command, carrying more than 95 percent of all equipment and supplies needed to sustain the war effort.*

ABOVE: *On board modern Aegis destroyers like the USS ARLEIGH BURKE, missiles transported in sealed canisters are loaded by crane directly into vertical launchers.* OPPOSITE PAGE: *On board the guided missile frigate the USS STEPHEN W. GROVES (FFG-29), the weapons department must schedule planned routine maintenance on each missile. Mold or the slightest corrosion can affect the operation and accuracy of the weapon.* OVERLEAF: *Information rich — the Combat Information Center (CIC) on board the USS TICONDEROGA (CG-47), first ship in a class of Aegis guided missile cruisers.* PAGES 50–51: *Time lapse photography of a standard missile launched from the Aegis cruiser the USS LAKE CHAMPLAIN (CG-57). Brian Wolff's camera took 65 frames per second. What is depicted in these images (every third frame) is the distance the missile traveled in a second.*

OPPOSITE AND ABOVE: *Two different views of a multiple missile launch aboard the Aegis destroyer USS COLE (DDG-67) operating in the Caribbean Sea.*

OPPOSITE AND ABOVE: *Depending on the cargo and volume being transferred, vertical replenishment adds speed and flexibility to the equation.*

OVERLEAF: *An SH-2 Sea Sprite helicopter, assigned to HSL-37, approaches the USS TICONDEROGA from the stern. This versatile helo has a variety of missions including anti-submarine, search and rescue, cargo transfer, medical evacuation, personnel and cargo transfer, boat interdiction, gunfire spotting, mine detection and battle damage assessment.*

PAGES 58–59: *Known as HIFR, or Helicopter In-flight Refueling, an SH-3 Sea King helicopter prepares to receive aviation gas without taking the time to land on the deck of the USS HAYLER.*

TOP LEFT: *A Sailor is lowered to the deck from an SH-3 helicopter;* TOP CENTER AND TOP RIGHT: *SH-60 Sea Hawk helicopters like this one are used for search and rescue, drug interdiction, cargo lift, anti-ship warfare and more.* ABOVE: *Sonobuoys are loaded aboard an SH-60 in preparation for its anti-submarine warfare mission.* RIGHT: *With collapsible rotors and tail, the SH-2 Sea Sprite helicopter can be stored in the hangar of this guided missile frigate.*

These pages show three views of an Aegis cruiser: High-tech engineering control room; a Sailor performs routine maintenance on a gas turbine generator; ships like this are capable of supporting carrier battle groups, amphibious forces, or of operating independently. In support of anti-submarine warfare (ASW), this ship is employing "senuous course steering" (frequent, slow course changes) to inhibit a submarine's ability to effectively target the ship and obtain a fire control solution. Every ship has a unique "signature" based on her engine, propeller, hull shape, and more. To add to the confusion of any aggressor submarine, ships can reduce their propeller and engine noises (known as Prairie Masker) to make them more difficult to detect by acoustic systems (sonar).

SAR Operations Require Teamwork

"Two hundred miles east of Virginia Beach, and bound for Norfolk, a 2,000 ton collier, "Golden Sea" sent a distress signal that was intercepted by the U. S. Coast Guard Fifth District Headquarters in Portsmouth, Virginia. A crewman had suffered multiple stab wounds to the stomach and was in a critical condition.

The Coast Guard contacted the Search and Rescue (SAR) Detachment at Naval Air Station Oceana and offered to escort the Navy's UH-3H SAR helo, with a Coast Guard C-130 Hercules out of Elizabeth City, North Carolina. I enthusiastically accepted their offer before launching "Rescue 725" in gusty winds. Once we were airborne, the two aircraft established communications before encountering 60-knot headwinds, low visibility and a low ceiling just 10 miles off the coast.

The Coast Guard established communications with Golden Sea and received an updated ship's position. Buffeted by strong headwinds, I knew I didn't have enough fuel to complete the mission. Fortunately for me — and the injured crewman — the aircraft carrier USS JOHN C. STENNIS (CVN-74) was within 50 miles of the distressed ship but could not launch helicopters in the strong wind. However, the ship did offer to tank me for the return leg back to Oceana.

With valuable help from the Coast Guard's onboard radar, the Hercules crew vectored me directly to Golden Sea. The ship maintained a steady course and speed while I hovered amidships into the 50-knot wind — in effect backing down while the Golden Sea drove into the helicopter.

My rescue swimmer, Petty Officer August Anstatt, was hoisted to the deck of Golden Sea and quickly evaluated the patient, determining that he was close to lapsing into shock. Without delay, my swimmer loaded the patient into a litter and they both were hoisted up to my chopper. While enroute to the carrier the patient lapsed into shock and my crewman administered first aid.

We alerted the aircraft carrier of our patient's condition before an uneventful landing. The medical team on board STENNIS determined that the patient required emergency surgery to preserve his life, so took him immediately to the ship's hospital for treatment. He remained overnight for observation and was taken to a Virginia Beach hospital two days later. After refueling, we launched for the return flight to NAS Oceana. In just over five hours, "Rescue 725" had completed another successful mission with a happy ending."

— Lieutenant John Higgins, U.S. Navy
SAR Detachment, NAS Oceana

THESE PAGES: *Hauling lines proves good exercise for the ARLEIGH BURKE Sailors; getting one's sea legs takes time, but after you've been underway for a while, leaning into the wind and walking "crooked" becomes second nature; deck seamanship includes learning how to flake a line (to coil it so it runs without knotting). The coast of Chile, with its snow-capped mountains and rich vegetation offers the team a rewarding view.*

"There's something truly special about the 0400 to 0800 watch when you're at sea. As an Officer of the Deck aboard destroyers in the Atlantic, it was always my favorite. Maybe it was the camaraderie of the watch team — a helmsman from my hometown, or a quartermaster elated that his morning star fix confirmed the ship's position as calculated by satellite navigation. Perhaps it was the surge of adrenalin when the ship lost all steering control, followed by a sense of relief that I had taken effective action in response to the surprise steering casualty drill conducted by the Operations Officer. Maybe it was being greeted by a gorgeous sunrise and stepping out on the bridge wing to listen to the cries of a lone seagull, to discover that we'd been steaming in the company of a school of bottle-nosed dolphins. Maybe it was listening to the Boatswainmate of the Watch conduct reveille over the 1 MC internal communications circuit and hearing the ship spring to life. I guess it must have been a combination of all those things. What I do remember is that I was always ravenous after getting relieved from the 04–08 watch, and after a large, delicious breakfast, I always felt invigorated, refreshed and ready to tackle the day's problems."

— A Surface Warfare Officer

NATO's Standing Naval Force Atlantic

The Standing Naval Force Atlantic is a unique naval entity. Its roots go back to 1960 when it was proposed that a NATO Anti-Submarine Warfare Task Group be formed. By 1963 discussions had progressed and a suggestion was put forward that an extended international exercise be conducted for a small NATO task group of four to six frigates. In early 1965, Canada, the Netherlands, the United Kingdom, and the United States each committed one ship for a five-month series of exercises known as Matchmaker I. The success of these exercises was followed by Matchmaker II in 1966 and Matchmaker III in 1967. Meanwhile, the idea of a permanent "Matchmaker" squadron was attracting attention. The Standing Naval Force Atlantic (STANAVFORLANT) was approved by the North Atlantic Counsel in December 1967, and it came into being on January 13, 1968, in a short ceremony in Portland, UK. It became the world's first permanent, multi-national naval squadron operating in peacetime.

The squadron is comprised of from five to nine destroyer or frigate type ships operating continuously as a single unit. Ships are provided by the NATO navies normally operating in the Atlantic Ocean and are assigned to STANAVFORLANT for two to six months. Under the NATO pennant, the squadron carries out a program of scheduled national and international exercises and maneuvers. The combined force also makes port visits to coastal cities of NATO member nations. In a typical year, the force will steam more than 50,000 miles, and visit more than 25 ports in 11 countries.

STANAVFORLANT is a bold example of international fellowship and cooperation among nations. The ships' crews perfect the techniques of operating together by constant practice between ships, and by personnel exchanges within the force. The mission of this force is defined by four basic objectives: It demonstrates the solidarity and cohesiveness of the Alliance with ships of member nations operating continuously as a single force. It provides an immediately available naval force capable of rapid deployment to a threatened area in times of crisis or tension. It provides a core element around which a more powerful naval force could be built. It improves NATO teamwork through training and experience.

Although French and English are the official NATO languages, the spoken language in the force is English. Most officers and senior ratings of the north European allies are highly proficient in English. The universal common language, which is well understood in the force, is the unspoken language of the mariner; and understanding and respect for the sea builds a common bond among those assigned to the Standing Naval Force Atlantic.

Unity Within the Americas

The men on watch on the bridge of the destroyer USS HAYLER breathe a collective sigh of relief as the Chilean pilot steps on board and relieves the Officer of the Deck. In a quiet voice filled with the confidence born of experience and skill, he issues rudder and engine orders to the ship's helmsman and lee helmsman. HAYLER'S bow slices cleanly through the ink-black waters of the narrow, twisting channel. On either side, steep evergreen walls rise out of the water, turn to stone, and disappear in the fog. Passage through this inland waterway around the southernmost end of South America is a voyage filled with majestic, snow-capped peaks, with channels so narrow it appears impossible our ship can pass. With its hundreds of tiny islands and tortuous channels, the Strait of Magellan connects the Atlantic and Pacific Oceans. The interior is a wild land of mountains and vast ranges of conifers. The region is legend to ships' navigators and quartermasters because maneuvering here takes superior skill, and undivided attention, perhaps made the more difficult by the distractions of the raw beauty of nature.

We've just completed training with the Chilean Navy and after passing through the Strait of Magellan, ships of the force will turn North for a seven-day liberty call in the year-round festival atmosphere of Rio de Janeiro, Brazil.

For 38 years Unitas has stood as a symbol of friendship and cooperation between the nations involved. Equally important, it is a visible demonstration of the ability and willingness of the nations involved to work together, to set aside any differences, and recognize a mutual goal — the common defense of mutual interests in this hemisphere.

President John F. Kennedy once said, "Let us not be blind to our differences — but let us also direct our attention to our common interests and the means by which those differences can be resolved. And if we cannot end now our differences, at least we can help make the world safe for diversity."

Unitas was born in 1959 from a suggestion made by some South American officers attending a U.S. Navy-hosted conference. That conference was intended to produce recommendations on the role of U.S. naval missions to the respective countries in South America. One of the recommendations was that the United States Navy send units to each of

PRECEDING PAGES: *The USS HAYLER transits the Strait of Magellan.*
BELOW: *The guided missile cruiser USS JOSEPHUS DANIELS (CG-23) rounds one of hundreds of tiny islands that make navigating the Strait of Magellan a challenge.*
LEFT: *A quartermaster checks his chart with the beam of a flashlight. While steaming at night, a ship's bridge must remain dark — even a short burst of brilliant light would render watchstanders temporarily blind, jeopardizing the safety of the ship.*
OPPOSITE: *Local Chilean fishermen exchange crabs for cigarettes with the crew of the guided missile frigate USS STEPHEN W. GROVES.*

the countries for the purpose of mutually beneficial, bilateral naval exercises. That early willingness to participate in multilateral naval operations and training was welcomed as an encouraging sign of greater friendship and a spirit of cooperation within the hemisphere.

That first Unitas lasted 102 days, with three weeks of bilateral and multilateral exercises. A total of 48 ships from Argentina, Brazil, Colombia, Ecuador, Uruguay, Venezuela, and the United States participated. Since then, the annual training exercise has grown to nearly five months, with more than 75 days of multilateral exercises, involving nearly three score ships, more than 100 aircraft, and 14,000 Sailors and Marines. Now Unitas involves more than just at sea exercises. It offers an opportunity for amphibious operations, special warfare, and aviation cross-training.

The benefits of such exercises go far beyond the opportunity to conduct naval exercises with our South American allies. Nearly half the time is spent in port, where lasting friendships can begin. Sailors routinely go out into the local community to meet with students, compete in international athletic competition, and repair, maintain, or construct local schools, churches, and housing projects. The professional exchange, coordinated training, and goodwill resulting from Unitas make this annual exercise extremely popular among U.S. Navy Sailors and their South American counterparts.

LEFT: *Although 16-hour days and longer are routine aboard deployed ships, often there is a well-deserved break. Shown here are Sailors on board the USS ARLEIGH BURKE enjoying a "Steel Beach Barbecue."*

BELOW: *Sailors play Hackey Sack — if it goes out of bounds (and over the side) the game is over.*

OPPOSITE TOP: *One of the more popular diversions is Swim Call. Here, a Midshipman on his summer cruise takes a break from his studies.*

OPPOSITE BOTTOM: *Sailors are experts at improvisation. When they are away from their favorite gym they can still get a good workout.*

OPPOSITE, TOP: *Whether at sea or in port, there are always watches to stand. Having the watch to ring in the New Year can be rewarding — for decades there have been contests for the best poem written and submitted by New Year's Eve watchstanders. Winning entries are published in ship and station newspapers and other publications.*

OPPOSITE, BOTTOM: *Sailors on board the guided missile cruiser USS TICONDEROGA ceremoniously conduct evening colors and fold the American flag.*

RIGHT: *Sailors on board the Second Fleet flagship USS MOUNT WHITNEY (LCC-20) wave goodbye as the ship leaves Norfolk.*

BELOW: *Underway replenishment at night presents unique hazards, including of course the possibility of man overboard.*

OPPOSITE: *An aerial view of the guided missile frigate USS STEPHEN W. GROVES. Procured in the mid-1970s and 1980s, guided missile frigates of this class were intended to counter the Soviet submarine threat. With limited anti-air warfare capabilities, their utility in a shrinking Navy is questionable. Of the 51 OLIVER HAZARD PERRY-class frigates, many have already been turned over to the Naval Reserve Force for training. As more Aegis destroyers join the fleet, these ships will be retired.*

Two sticking points. ABOVE: *One of the most prestigious accomplishments for junior officers and petty officers is the hard-earned Surface Warfare pin. Many say it is more important than rank in commanding respect and credibility.* RIGHT: *A Sailor with chronic seasickness is treated by the ship's hospital corpsman. If it can't be controlled, seasickness can be debilitating and the service member will be discharged.*

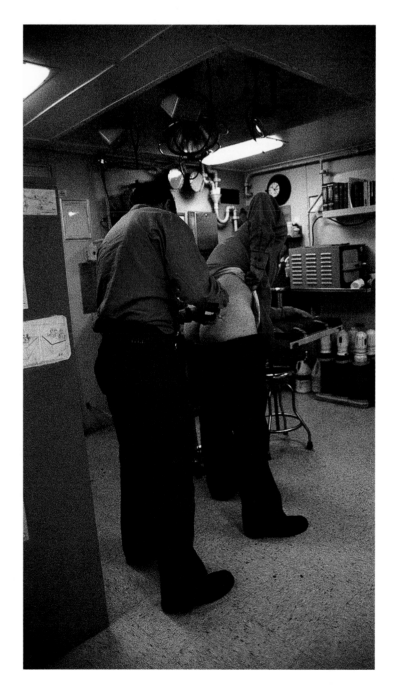

OPPOSITE AND TOP: *The USS THE SULLIVANS (DDG-68), named to honor five brothers who lost their lives while serving together on board the cruiser USS JUNEAU (CL-52) at the Battle of Guadalcanal, steams into New York harbor for her commissioning ceremony in April 1997.* ABOVE: *Wearing seven gold stripes on his sleeve to indicate 28 years of experience, it's easy to see why these USS TICONDEROGA Sailors listen attentively to their Command Master Chief.*

ABOVE: *The frigate USS CAPODANNO.* OPPOSITE, TOP: *Chief Boatswainmate (SW) Veda L. Brown commands the tugboat MENOMINEE (YT-790) in Hampton Roads, Virginia, one of the busiest Navy ports in the world.* OPPOSITE, BOTTOM: *Chief Brown's crew watches as the USS MILWAUKEE (AOR-2) returns to Norfolk.*

Unless you've been separated from your family for a minimum of six months, and missed the birth of your child, it is hard to imagine the elation of being reunited with family and loved ones, and the sheer joy of seeing your new infant for the first time. These Sailors have "been there; done that!"

NAVAL AVIATION
Wings of Gold

High Flight —
High Drama —
High Stakes

"Jet engines roar, catapults scream and hiss, exhaust gases and the smell of jet fuel overpower the salt air, and the flight deck is a flurry of organized chaos. There's something about strapping on more than 72,000 pounds of fire-breathing hardware, roaring off into the heavens and defying the laws of gravity. I can't help but marvel at the power and lethality that my country has entrusted to me — this nearly 62-foot-long jet that costs more than $38 million. One forward motion from my gloved hand kicks in the afterburners, and soon I'm out-racing my own sound. Faster than a .45 caliber bullet I can go straight up or straight down. I am a naval aviator and I am in complete control. It is not often that reality actually exceeds your dreams: but it certainly did for me.

Any time a couple of naval aviators get together the subject of night carrier landings is bound to come up. Is it as hard as everyone says? No. It's at least twice that hard! We have an image to uphold, so we don't talk about it much with outsiders. More pilots lose their wings because of their night time landing performance than for all of the other reasons combined. Day traps are fun. We'd do them for free and can't get enough of them. The same goes for daytime catapult shots. They're invigorating. But turn out the sun, obscure the horizon with a low ceiling and bad visibility; nobody likes that. Add a pitching deck and a thunderstorm; it's like practicing bleeding. Any pilot who doesn't dread landing on such a night is either kidding himself or not being truthful with you.

I'll never forget one particular black night like that. A squadronmate of mine was having difficulty getting aboard. He had so many looks at the pitching deck that he had to be tanked (inflight refueled) twice, along with a couple of other guys who were having similar problems. Finally, everyone, including the tanker, was safely aboard but him. On the ninth pass, he landed fine but his hook skipped the wires for a bolter. The tenth time he was high and fast all the way, another bolter. Each approach required so much concentration and effort that his strength, along with his chances of getting aboard safely, deteriorated each time he went around.

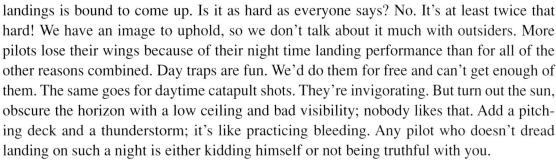

PRECEDING PAGES: *At the conclusion of flight operations, the last plane to land on board the USS SARATOGA (CV-60) is the Search and Rescue (SAR) helicopter.*

OPPOSITE: *An F/A-18 Hornet is waved off from landing on board the USS AMERICA.*
ABOVE: *Wearing chains is second nature to this USS JOHN F. KENNEDY (CV-67) plane captain. The chains are used to secure "his" plane to the flight deck.*

While flying downwind to set up for his eleventh pass, thoughts of his wife and son flashed through his mind. He was convinced he'd never see them again because the sea was too rough and too cold for a rescue. He was low, the deck was coming up. The Landing Signals Officer (LSO) waved him off at the last second, narrowly averting disaster. This was "blue water ops;" no divert fields to escape the blackness. Somehow, somewhere, he mustered all his remaining skill, courage, and concentration, and on that twelfth and final pass, the wire jerked him mercifully to a halt.

Every tailhooker has his "turn in the barrel" sooner or later. You just have to take a deep breath and try to convince yourself, 'What doesn't kill you makes you tougher.' That particular pilot flew superbly the rest of the cruise and was a great LSO on the next one. He went on to be an instructor teaching young pilots how to land aboard a carrier — even became commanding officer of one of our Navy's newest aircraft carriers."

— An F-14 Pilot and former Top Gun Instructor

USS SARATOGA flight operations. OPPOSITE, TOP AND ABOVE: *An F/A-18 Hornet.* OPPOSITE, BOTTOM: *An E-2C Hawkeye early warning aircraft — the "Eyes and Ears of the fleet."*

THESE PAGES: *F-14 Tomcats like the one above launching from the USS GEORGE WASHINGTON (CVN-73), or the one at rest on board the USS DWIGHT D. EISENHOWER (CVN-69), can track up to 24 enemy aircraft simultaneously, operating around the clock.*

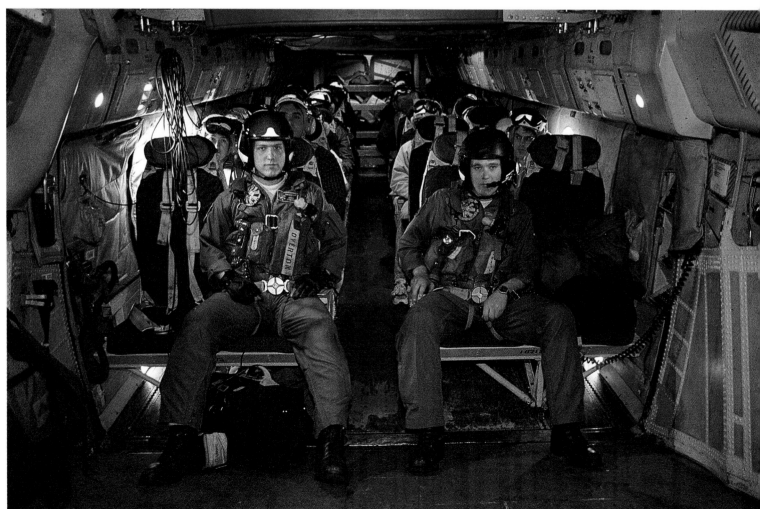

THESE PAGES: *The C-2A Greyhound provides critical logistics support to aircraft carriers. The cabin is designed to accommodate cargo (like spare parts and mail) and passengers. It is also equipped to accept litter patients in support of medical evacuation missions. It isn't a luxury airliner, but an invaluable utilitarian workhorse. From November 1985 to February 1987, Reserve Squadron VR-24, operating with seven C-2As, demonstrated exceptional operational readiness while delivering two million pounds of cargo, two million pounds of mail, and 14,000 passengers in support of the European and Mediterranean theaters.*

OVERLEAF: *Inside the Combat Direction Center (CDC) on board the USS THEODORE ROOSEVELT (CVN-71), all ships, aircraft, and missiles are plotted automatically for instant reference and rapid response.*

Training Makes Us One Navy

"I take up my pen and write a stark entry in my journal: "Welcome to the war." I have just returned from my first combat mission as a Naval Reserve combat crewmember, dropping MK-82 bombs on enemy targets. It's early 1991 and the Persian Gulf conflict is still raging. I am the commanding officer of Attack Squadron augmentation unit 0686 stationed out of Naval Air Station Oceana, in Virginia Beach, Virginia. Ours was the only medium attack Naval Reserve augmentation unit on the East Coast when the war broke out, and 18 of us were selected for mobilization in a combat status. I'm stationed on board the USS THEODORE ROOSEVELT in the Persian Gulf. I'm wondering how three of my squadron personnel are making out: Petty Officer First Class Walter Thompson, on board the USS MIDWAY(CV-41); Petty Officer Second Class Jim Maxey on board the USS JOHN F. KENNEDY; and Lieutenant Commander Kevin Lyles, who is somewhere in the Gulf protecting Navy minesweepers.

Just days before I was an investment counselor, Walt a policeman, Jim a grocery store clerk, and Kevin a teacher. Wrenching a diverse group like us out of our comfortable civilian jobs, catapulting us to the other side of the world, and putting us in harm's way is the sort of situation that a TV writer might have dreamed up as the plot for a new sitcom.

Since the Total Force Concept was inaugurated in the early 1970s, reserve units have had to meet the same training requirements, have used the same equipment, and have been subject to the same standards of readiness as a comparable regular unit. It is a bold idea. It assumes that given the right kind of leadership, a reserve unit can approach, perhaps even achieve, the same level of combat readiness as a regular unit — and at a lower cost. But at this point, the concept has not been tested in the crucible of a real war. Will it work?

I am confident that it will. 0686 has aggressively sought joint training with fleet squadrons. The year before, we logged nearly 1,700 A-6 hours, 70 percent of them flown with active-duty squadrons. Just prior to being deployed in the Gulf region, we conducted training with Attack Squadron 75 that included coordinated heavy-ordnance strikes against opposed targets, day and night low-level flying, and new night-bombing tactics.

In the days and weeks that followed our mobilization, we did just that. When we

pooled our individual stories later on, we found that we had compiled a record our unit would be proud of. Of the three friends I mentioned earlier, here is how our individual stories turned out: Walt Thompson reported on board MIDWAY on 1 February 1991. Within one week he was placed in charge of all flight-deck ordnance operations and was later awarded a Navy Achievement Medal.

Jim Maxey was employed rearming F-14s on board the USS JOHN F. KENNEDY. Although his experience up to that time had been limited to the A-6 aircraft, he was up to speed in no time. Jim later received a letter of commendation from the ship's captain. LCDR Kevin Lyles was awarded the Navy Commendation Medal with combat "V" for defending mine countermeasures forces clearing Iraqi mines from Kuwait's coastal waters.

As for me, I flew a total of 15 combat and/or combat support missions over Iraq and Kuwait. And I can tell you that the first time I saw anti-aircraft artillery fire streaking past my Intruder, I was very glad that we had taken combat readiness seriously.

The Naval Reserve Unit identified as VA-0686 was recognized by naval leadership as having significantly enhanced the ability of the Medium Attack Wing One (MATWINGONE) to meet its Gulf War commitments. Speaking for all of us who served, I can say that we are proudest of the accolade bestowed by MATWINGONE commanding officer: "There is no difference between the regular and the reserve Navy with the volunteers of VA-0686 . . . I view them as combat assets first."

— Commander Thomas C. Stewart, USNR-R

OPPOSITE: *An A-6 Intruder launches from the USS SARATOGA with an F/A-18 Hornet ready to go. First introduced in 1960, the highly capable Intruder worked around the clock in Vietnam, and they were used extensively during the Gulf War.* ABOVE: *On board the USS AMERICA (CV-66) an EA-6B Prowler and a CH-53 Sea Stallion go from the flight deck to the hangar deck on an elevator.*

PRECEDING PAGES: *A Sailor begins his day at sea on board the USS AMERICA cleaning the canopy of an F-14 to ensure perfect visibility.* OPPOSITE TOP: *The ordnancemen inspect a laser-guided bomb on board the USS CONSTELLATION (CV-64).* OPPOSITE BOTTOM: *Flight deck noise can be deafening. Ear protection worn by this Sailor on board the USS INDEPENDENCE (CV-62) permits him to hear shouting voices above the roar of jet exhaust and engines.* TOP OF PAGE: *Residue from mulched classified material.* ABOVE: *Sophisticated flight simulators, complete with intelligence briefings, allow pilots to "fly" their mission before they ever launch from the carrier.*

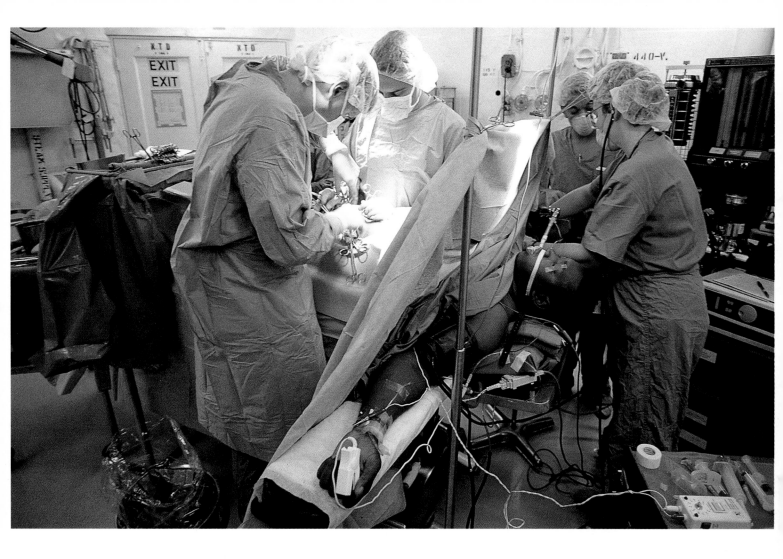

OPPOSITE TOP: *During a break in flight deck operations, this jogger on board the USS SARATOGA makes good use of the 4.5 acres to keep physically fit.* OPPOSITE BOTTOM: *Sorting and distributing tons of mail is a full-time job on board the USS JOHN F. KENNEDY.* TOP: *Carrier Battle Groups take their own hospital with them. This surgical wing on board the USS SARATOGA is equipped with state-of-the-art technology.* ABOVE: *With a crew and embarked wing of more than 5,000, the USS CARL VINSON' barber still makes time for good customer relations.*

OVERLEAF: *This S-3A Viking is designed to hunt and destroy enemy submarines and provide surveillance of surface shipping.*

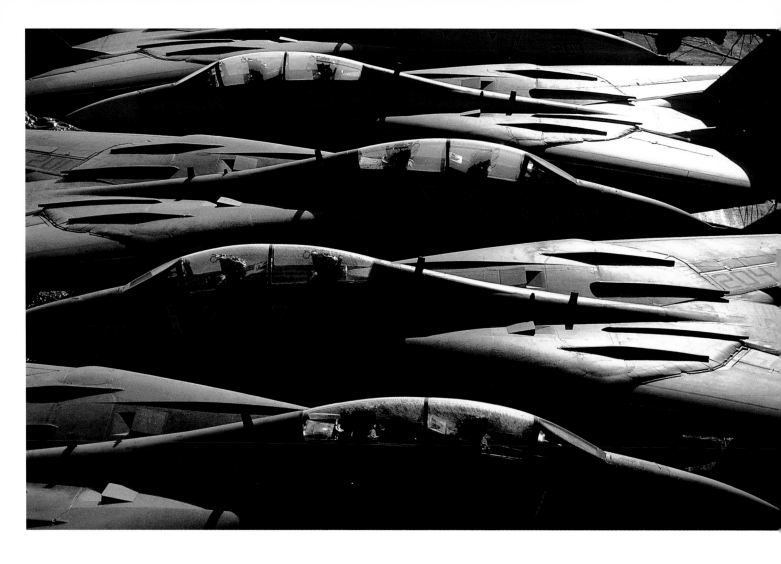

TOP: *A flock of F-14 Tomcats rest comfortably on board the USS JOHN F. KENNEDY.* ABOVE: *On board the USS CONSTELLATION (CV-64), this green shirt indicates all systems go for the next catapult launch.* OPPOSITE, TOP: *A handler on board the USS THEODORE ROOSEVELT keeps track of every plane in the air and on the deck to ensure safety during flight operations.* OPPOSITE, BOTTOM: *Ordnancemen on board the USS INDEPENDENCE inspect a Sidewinder air-to-air missile.*

OPPOSITE: *The multi-mission F/A-18 Hornet is both a fighter and an attack air-craft, capable of carrying 17,000 pounds of ordnance, including Sparrow, Harm, Harpoon, and Sidewinder missiles. These aircraft flew nearly 10,000 Navy and Marine Corps missions during Operation Desert Storm.* ABOVE: *A Sailor makes final preparations for the launch of an E-2C Hawkeye from the USS SARATOGA. This plane is known as the "eyes and ears of the fleet," providing all-weather airborne early warning and command and control functions for the battle group.*

Searching for Submarines
in the North Atlantic

"I woke to the sound of my alarm clock amidst the quiet darkness of my Bachelor Officer Quarters. Moments later my fellow crew members knock on my door, ready to begin the day. We step outside to wait for the squadron duty driver and are greeted by a nasty mix of frigid wind and drifting snow. The duty driver arrives and we join our enlisted crew mates to begin an unknown journey.

Our crew files past the armed Marine guard and down the halls of hardened bunkers to the briefing room. Under dim lights the briefing officer informs us of the day's requirements. We are to patrol the North Atlantic in search of a CIS submarine. The intelligence is limited and the location uncertain. Our job: locate the submarine and maintain its track. A long half-hour later we depart the briefing room, retrace our steps along the hardened concrete walls, past the Marine, and rejoin our duty driver.

At the hangar, each crew member inspects and dons his and her personal survival vests, grabs any tools necessary for the flight mission and departs the hangar. As I pass through the small opening in the hangar door, I am embraced by the all too familiar Icelandic wind. My head tucked down into my parka hood, I push through the howling wind and horizontal-blowing snow, shuffling my feet carefully to maneuver across three-inch-thick ice to the mighty gray aircraft across the apron. It is thirty years old, older than most of the air crews that now

fly it, but that's proof of its durability and trustworthiness. Although considered a dinosaur by some, this all-weather aircraft stands at the technological forefront of the anti-submarine world, capable of tracking submarines via sonobuoys and magnetic anomaly detections with the most sophisticated equipment. Capabilities also include infra-red and electronic surveillance, as well as forward firing anti-ship weapons.

As I enter the aircraft, I am greeted by the smiling faces of my flight engineers who have already fueled the aircraft and heated the interior to a comfortable 70 degrees F. I make my way to the front and stow my gear at the Tactical Coordinator station. All hands commence their preflight routine, working diligently to ensure an on-time takeoff. They know our squadron mates are already there searching, hundreds of miles off the coast, depending on us to relieve them.

The preflight complete, we assemble aft for the plane-side brief. With game faces on now, the pilots brief safety of flight aspects, the navigator briefs the route of the flight, and I brief our tactical mission. Twelve months of grueling simulators, classes, meetings, and qualification flights come together for this single, nine-hour flight. The pressure is visible on our faces knowing that the eyes of the world will read our debrief tomorrow.

After the plane-side debrief, everyone goes to their assigned stations and the flight station begins the engine start checklist. Number two propeller slowly spins into a circular blur, followed in succession by the remaining three engines. Loaded with 80 sonobuoys, we taxi cautiously across the patches of ice to the cleared runway. Moments later we are airborne. The sun peeks above the horizon as we pass over the frozen volcanic island and out over the blue-purple sea. We journey far into the North Atlantic, patrolling the skies to locate and track every ship and submarine that passes through the Greenland-Iceland-United Kingdom Gap. Few people even know we are out here. But we are."

— Lieutenant Travis White is an Instructor Naval Flight Officer stationed at VP-30, the Fleet Readiness Squadron at NAS Jacksonville, Florida.

ABOVE: *Before flight operations can begin, flight deck crewmembers conduct a Foreign Object Damage (FOD) walk down. Anything loose on deck can be disastrous if sucked into a jet engine. Such walk downs are conducted periodically throughout the aircraft operations cycle.*

OPPOSITE: *Like her namesake, the USS CONSTELLATION has a long and proud record of service. Commissioned on October 27, 1961, her 36 years of service have included time on Yankee Station off the coast of Vietnam, and in the Gulf of Oman in the Arabian Sea. Four arresting wires are used to "trap" returning aircraft. The aircraft's tailhook engages one of the four wires which pulls the aircraft to an abrupt stop. Aircraft landing at speeds up to 180 miles per hour are brought to a halt in about 300 feet. When operating with Harriers, the USS CONSTELLATION removes the arresting gear wires since the Harriers launch and land vertically, without the aid of catapults or arresting wires. Harrier pilots attached to the 15th Marine Expeditionary Unit landed on the USS CONSTELLATION's flight deck, working to improve joint operations capabilities.*

OVERLEAF: *The EA-6B Prowler like this one on board the USS SARATOGA, provides an umbrella of protection over strike aircraft and ships by jamming enemy radar, electronic data links, and communications.*

PAGES 118–119: *Night launch of an F-14 Tomcat from the USS THEODORE ROOSEVELT.*

OPPOSITE, TOP: *The catapult control station on the forward flight deck of the USS SARATOGA. Steam from the previous launch is still rising.* OPPOSITE, BOTTOM: *SH-3 Sea King ASW helicopters like this one on board the USS EISENHOWER employ variable depth sonar, sonobuoys, data link and chaff (foil strips to confuse enemy radar systems).* ABOVE: *An aircraft on the glide path is watched closely by the Landing Signals Officer (LSO). He holds high his "wave off" light switch to show pri-fly that he's sent the plane back around for another pass.* OVERLEAF: *An F-14 Tomcat and an F/A-18 Hornet from the USS INDEPENDENCE enjoy the view from above the clouds.* PAGES 124–125: *At sunset, a yellow shirt plane handler on board the USS CARL VINSON conducts a critically important part of the "ballet" that characterizes flight deck operations.*

"I'm a Yellow Shirt. When a plane is in rotation to be the next to launch, I direct it to the catapult. After it traps, I direct it to the proper place on the flight deck. There are five or six like me in each of the three fly areas. A good aircraft director doesn't care what type of plane he directs, he gets proficient in all of them. There is constant danger on the flight deck. You can get sucked in, run over, blown over, knocked down. I've had warm jet wash hit me at knee level and blow me through the air ten feet before I could grab onto something.

To stay sharp we have fire drills every couple days. There are so many fire hazards on a flight deck — burning metal, toxic fumes, overheated weapons, exhaust fuel, electrical cables. Exhaust from a jet can ignite something, or fuel on the deck can catch on fire and travel down a catapult. We practice charging the fire, knocking it down, cooling the weapons. If a fire last even a minute, we're in big trouble. Eighteen hour days are long, but I think I have the best job on the ship. Of course it's lonely on cruise. All you see is men. I tune in music and shut out the world, get in a zone and the days pass pretty quickly. Often I don't even know what day of the week or month it is."

— A Third Class Petty Officer

SUBMARINES
The Silent Workhorses

"Fast attack submarines gather intelligence, pursue enemy submarines, support carrier battle groups, and deliver men for special operations. We work in virtual isolation, cut off from fresh air and sunshine for months on end. Our only contact with the outside world is through our instruments. The work is arduous, in confined spaces, where the crew spends seven days a week, months on end until the boat surfaces again. The crew's only recreation area is on the mess decks. That's where sailors write letters, study, read books, play cards, and occasionally watch movies or a videotaped sporting event. Of course it's also where the crew dines. The food on submarines is considered the best in the Navy. It has a direct impact on morale.

Submariners work in a demanding, harsh environment where nothing can afford to be taken for granted. Submariners are a very unique, special group of people. They travel in and out of port unnoticed, transit to far away places and experience adventures they can't even discuss when they return home. Submariners go through extensive screening and difficult schools. The community attracts, and accepts only the brightest individuals. All are volunteers. Discipline is seldom a problem. Leading them is tremendously gratifying and rewarding. Watching them grow and excel is a marvelous benefit of command. Keeping them motivated is my highest priority and my most demanding constant challenge."

— A LOS ANGELES-class Submarine Skipper

PREVIOUS PAGES: *The USS HONOLULU (SSN-718) under way on the surface in the Pacific Ocean near her Pearl Harbor home port.*

OPPOSITE PAGE AND ABOVE: *The officer of the deck and the submarine's commanding officer scan the horizon through binoculars. On the surface, submarines usually are far less maneuverable and stable than when they are submerged.*

OVERLEAF: *The USS GEORGIA's 24 Trident missile hatches are open. The orange "bubbles" signify that the tubes are empty at the moment. By the turn of the century, the 18 Trident SSBNs will carry more than 50 percent of the total of U.S. strategic warheads.*

BELOW: *A view of the USS GEORGIA (SSBN-729) missile compartment. Deterrence of nuclear war has been the sole mission of the fleet ballistic missile submarine since its introduction to the fleet in 1960. As one of the OHIO-class missile submarines designed as a replacement to the Poseidon submarines, the USS GEORGIA carries 24 Trident I missiles. Each missile is 34 feet long, weighs 73,000 pounds, and has a range up to 4,000 nautical miles. In 1990, beginning with the USS TENNESSEE (SSBN-734), these submarines carry Trident II missiles which are 10 feet longer, have a comparable range, but deliver a significantly greater payload.*

OPPOSITE, TOP: *The missile launch panel aboard the USS GEORGIA.*

OPPOSITE, BOTTOM: *He holds the fate of the world in his hands. Hardly. Actually this weapons officer holds the practice firing key to the submarine's missile system. On board our Trident submarines, and other weapons platforms, there are redundant safety systems designed to prevent inadvertent or willful detonation by a single individual.*

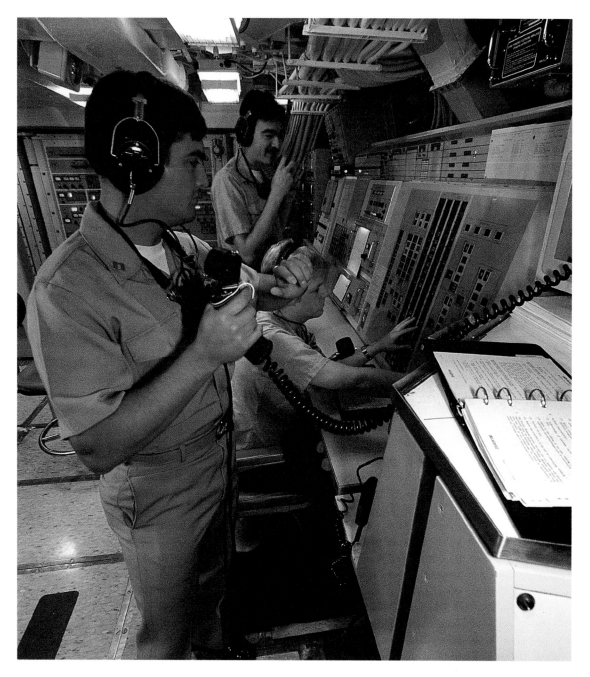

ABOVE: *The USS GEORGIA's ship's doctor takes air samples to ensure the confined environment has the right oxygen mix. Submarines make their own oxygen from distilled seawater. An oxygen generator breaks down the water into hydrogen (which is disposed of) and oxygen which is vented into the ship and stored in tanks. Navy doctors were once assigned to Trident submarines; today, Hospital Corpsmen are part of the crew.*OPPOSITE, TOP: *Main engineering control panel on board the USS GEORGIA.* OPPOSITE, BOTTOM: *The mess deck of a submarine serves as a dining room, work center, theater and lounge. They say there is no better food in the Navy than that served on board submarines.*

"We exist as a Navy to prevent conflict and to deter aggression. But sometimes aggression comes our way regardless of what we do. Then we exist to win in battle. That's when the most difficult circumstances arise. That's when the pressure is the greatest. That's when it isn't enough to survive; we must win and prevail. As a result, we train whenever we can. Because when that Tomahawk breaks the surface and heads ashore, it had better take out its objective. Many lives depend on it. When we lock that Harpoon on that combatant surface ship, it had better connect. He's not out there on a pleasure cruise. When we launch the torpedo, we had better get it on target. Aggressors shoot back. Minefields show no mercy and there is no second place. If the other guy does shoot, we had better be able to control the damage. You can't walk home. That's why we train — to compel the other side to our National will, to prevent him from aggressive action against the United States or our friends, and, failing that — to achieve victory in battle and allow us to experience a homecoming.

— Rear Admiral W. G. "Jerry" Ellis, USN
Commander, Submarine Force, U.S. Pacific Fleet

OPPOSITE: *The USS GEORIGA moored pierside at the Submarine Base in Kings Bay, Georgia.* ABOVE: *A Trident submarine crew prepares for quarters as the ship's commanding officer climbs onto the deck.*

OVERLEAF: *After surfacing near the North Pole, Sailors on board the LOS ANGELES-class attack submarine the USS SAN JUAN (SSN-751) clear ice from atop the sail in order to extend antennas to receive communications.*

ABOVE: *Security watches are common aboard submarines, but what makes them a bit more unusual near the Arctic Circle is the most common threat — polar bears.*

Surfacing at the Top of the World

The first question asked of submariners who have surfaced at the North Pole is usually, "How did you accomplish that feat?"

Here's the simple answer. Using special sonar, the submarine finds the thinnest ice. Some submarines have fairwater planes on the sail that can rotate to a vertical position to minimize stress and avoid damage as the submarine penetrates several feet of solid ice. Once the submarine is in position beneath the thinnest ice, the diving officer pumps out the ballast tanks and the submarine rises slowly but steadily, preventing damage to the sail and hull as the submarine breaks through the ice.

The second question — "Why do submariners want or need to surface inside the Arctic Circle?" — requires a more thoughtful and detailed response.

To find the answer we must go back some 40 years when Dr. Waldo Lyon, a bright, young physicist who founded the Navy's Arctic Submarine Laboratory in San Diego, provided direction to the USS NAUTILUS, the first submarine to ever transit beneath the ice cap in 1958. Throughout the Cold War (no reference here to the Arctic) frequent research trips to the north have been conducted to study the harsh and unforgiving environment. The body of collected knowledge has resulted in improvements in submarine design and tactics for their employment in northern climes. The answer then, is twofold: research and stealth, another clear example of naval forward deployment, in an almost extreme form.

A team of highly specialized scientists deployed from the San Diego facility are on hand with complex instrumentation to document precisely the tracks of the submarines, and to discover how the slab of ice responds to a jolt from below as the USS SAN JUAN and the USS PUFFER (SSN-62) slowly but surely break through the frozen medium. The results of their efforts can be valuable guidance on Arctic navigation to other submarine crews.

During this visit to the pole in 1994, the two submarines were testing and evaluating two different new sonar technologies. the USS SAN JUAN employed a computer-integrated sensor system designed to improve target tracking. the USS PUFFER used a super-computer which produced high-resolution sonar images, thus painting a detailed picture of the topography beneath the polar ice cap. Armed with this visual information, submarines can maneuver stealthily among underwater ice formations, identify targets, and view precisely where the ice cap is the thinnest. The system was impressive as pictures on these pages confirm. Armed with the new technology, Navy scientists can study the Arctic Ocean's floor, research this frigid battleground, and monitor the movement of the polar ice.

ABOVE: *The USS SAN JUAN receives a fresh supply of food delivered by a chartered aircraft.*

OPPOSITE TOP: *A sonar technician listens intently with equipment designed to work under the polar ice. With increased proficiency operating under the ice, our submarines are less vulnerable to detection and prosecution by anti-submarine aircraft and surface ships. Sonarmen identify and classify their contacts by listening to the sounds they emit. These sound "signatures" can be analyzed on a video screen and on computer print-outs. With experience and practice, a good sonar technician can identify contacts not simply by class of ship or submarine, but in some cases, even by specific unit.*

OPPOSITE BOTTOM: *Navigating through the ice is a unique challenge for the crew of the USS PUFFER. A STURGEON-class nuclear-powered attach submarine, the USS PUFFER is 292-feet long, has a beam of 32 feet, and displaces 4,640 tons submerged. Armed with Harpoon, Tomahawk, and Mark 48 torpedoes, this submarine carries a crew of 12 officers and 95 enlisted men.*

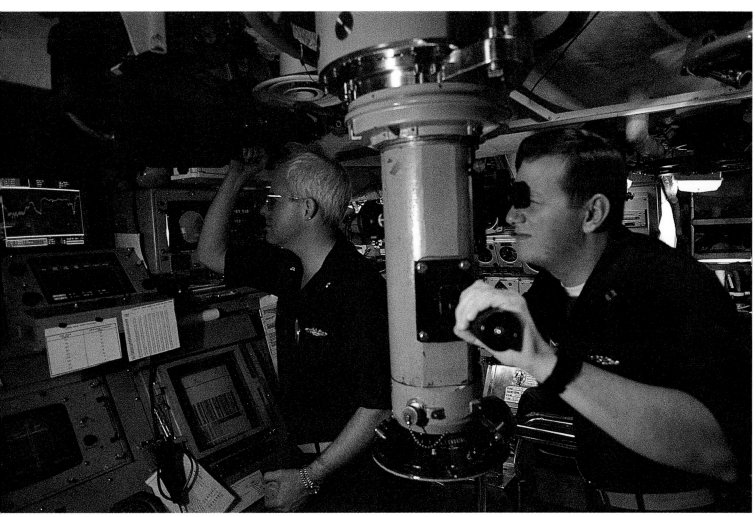

LEFT: *To these USS SAN JUAN Sailors, the Navy's Arctic Submarine Laboratory in San Diego must seem light-years away.*

BELOW: *After hearing that no one leaves the ice station alone, nor does any group venture out without a radio and gun because of polar bears, these USS PUFFER Sailors decide standing watch in the conning tower of the submarine isn't so bad after all.*

OPPOSITE: *Completely protected against the deadly arctic cold except for his eyes and mouth, this USS PUFFER Sailor may one day appreciate the significance of standing on top of the world.*

OPPOSITE, TOP: *The Applied Physics Laboratory Ice Station (APLIS) is a temporary camp managed for the Navy by the Applied Physics Laboratory of the University of Washington.*

OPPOSITE, CENTER: *Navy personnel at APLIS Command and Control Center conduct ice mechanics research as submarines surface at the pole, and analyze the effectiveness of new under-ice sonar equipment.*

OPPOSITE, BOTTOM: *Fresh-baked cookies are a popular item at the chow hut.*

ABOVE AND RIGHT: *On board the USS PUFFER, a new experimental sonar system uses a series of hydrophones and a computer to produce high resolution sonar images which outline the shape of the underside of the ice.*

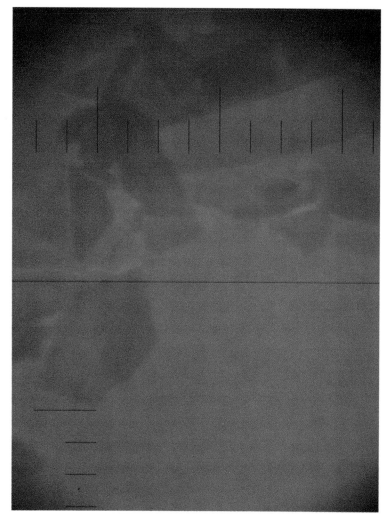

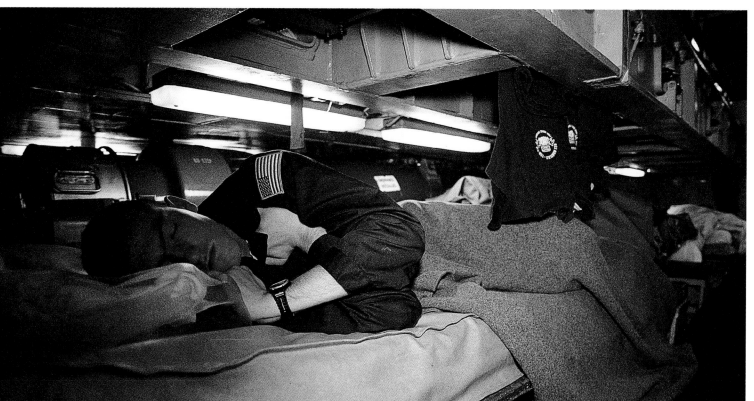

OPPOSITE: *At the Submarine Base in New London, Connecticut, submarine crews can get valuable training at this state-of-the-art simulator.* TOP LEFT: *A Sailor on board the USS HONOLULU wears thick rubber boots and dons rubber gloves before working on a live electrical panel. As a final safety precaution, a safety line is tied around his waist.* TOP RIGHT: *Mail is particularly welcome on board a submarine since these craft are capable of remaining submerged for months at a time.* ABOVE: *Sleeping compartments on board the USS HONOLULU give new meaning to the words cramped quarters. Although standard bunks measure 76 by 18 inches with overhead clearance of less than two feet, what is depicted here is a "skid rack" — temporary sleeping quarters next to torpedoes, that are used only when a submarine gets under way with more crew members than bunks.*

ABOVE: *Simulating severe damage, the USS HONOLULU conducts an emergency surfacing test. Compressed air is forced into the ballast tanks at thousands of pounds of pressure to raise the ship from a depth of several hundred feet.* BELOW LEFT: *Sailors receive a debrief following a damage control and firefighting drill.* BELOW RIGHT: *Aboard the USS PUFFER the crew literally lives on cans of food.*

ABOVE: *A floating dry dock crew receives a morning briefing before commencing the day's scheduled maintenance on board a submarine.* BELOW: *Control room on board the USS HYMAN G. RICKOVER (SSN-709). Under the supervision of the COB (Chief of the Boat), enlisted crewmembers stand watch at the helm and diving planes.*

ABOVE: *After torpedoes are loaded on board the USS HONOLULU by crane, they are guided down a hatch at an angle, tail first , and are secured in storage racks in the submarine's torpedo room.* OPPOSITE: *The USS HONOLULU steams on the surface. The interesting, not to say beautiful wake in the foreground is made by a helicopter hovering at low altitude, perhaps to execute a personnel transfer.*

ABOVE: *A technical representative is transferred to a tugboat to save this Trident submarine from having to return to port. This humanitarian evacuation or "HUMEVAC" was conducted off the coast of Bermuda when the submarine learned that family illness required the man's presence at home.* OPPOSITE: *The USS HONOLULU comes home to Pearl Harbor.*

PRECEDING PAGES: *At "Sniper School" at Marine Corps Base Quantico, Virginia, students, like this Marine, learn some of the skills they will put to use in carrying out clandestine, unconventional warfare missions.*

"Operating forward, in fully capable combined arms teams, the Marine Corps will be America's legion — on the scene, ever ready to protect the nation's interests. We will remain fundamentally naval and expeditionary in character, as comfortable on the seas as on the land and in the air. With the Navy, we will be able to go anywhere rapidly and project force across any shore against any foe, sustaining ourselves from the sea or land bases."

— General C.C. Krulak, Commandant of the Marine Corps

Pictures on these pages depict the deployment of the 26th Marine Expeditionary Unit, departing from Moorehead City, North Carolina.

OPPOSITE TOP: *The moment of truth — this young boy finally realizes his Dad is leaving on a long trip, and finds it difficult to maintain a stiff upper lip.*

OPPOSITE BOTTOM: *Try packing everything you'll need to be away from home for six months (including weather extremes), knowing that you'll be on board ship part of the time, sometimes at an established base camp, and at other times who knows where. Those seabags are heavy, too!*

ABOVE AND RIGHT: *Members of the 26th MEU on an LCU (Landing Craft Utility) that will take them to the amphibious assault ship USS NASSAU (LHA-4). While deployed to the Mediterranean, the 26th MEU participated in an evacuation from Albania. Before returning home, the Marines transferred to two other ships, the USS NASHVILLE (LPD-13) and the USS PENSACOLA (LSD-38).*

A Marine AV-8B Harrier jet flies over the snow-capped mountains of Norway during a cold weather exercise. This aircraft is the only vertical and short take-off (V/STOL) plane in the U.S. Armed Forces, and is used extensively to support amphibious operations, precisely because of its V/STOL capabilities.

A fully-loaded Landing Craft Air Cushion (LCAC) carrying trucks and tanks makes preparations to leave the well deck at the back of the USS BOXER (LHD-4), one of the largest amphibious ships in the world.

ABOVE: *Converted from an amphibious assault ship, the USS INCHON now serves as a mine countermeasures command, control and support vessel. With state-of-the-art communications, computers, and intelligence, the USS INCHON (MCS-12) provides the squadron commander with key mission planning, execution, and evaluation capabilities.* OPPOSITE, TOP: *A mine-hunting robot is lifted on board the USS SCOUT (MCM-8), a mine countermeasures ship. With a fiberglass-sheathed wooden hull and sophisticated automatic degaussing system, this class of ships has a very low magnetic signature.* OPPOSITE, BOTTOM: *The USS INCHON and the USS AVENGER (MCM-1) operate together. The larger ship can offer underway logistics and repair to forward-deployed mine countermeasures assets.*

The Mine Countermeasures Triad

In terms of cost-effectiveness and impact on the littoral environment, mines are the single most attractive weapon available to anyone intent on inhibiting the ability of U. S. Naval Forces to project power from the sea. Mine Countermeasures, therefore, are critical to the ability of naval forces to effectively shape and dominate the battle space. Mine countermeasures can be broken into three basic elements: surface, air, and explosive ordnance disposal (EOD) — known as the MCM Triad. These forces compliment each other in performing their missions.

Airborne mine countermeasures (AMCM) is conducted by MH-53E Sea Dragon helicopters, the largest helicopters in the Navy's inventory, which can carry a wide variety of mine detection equipment. The helicopters serve as the cavalry of mine countermeasures, quickly responding world-wide to any contingency. They provide commanders at sea with a flexible means of dealing with all mine threats. Explosive Ordnance Disposal (EOD) divers are flexible as well. EOD is deployable with the helicopters and ships, and provides the helicopters with a neutralization capability they lack when operating on their own.

OPPOSITE, TOP: *CH-46E Sea Knight Helicopters like the ones on board the USS NASSAU are used by the Marine Corps to provide all-weather, day or night assault transport of combat troops, supplies and equipment.* OPPOSITE, BOTTOM: *A CH-53 Sea Stallion helicopter rests in the shadows on the hangar deck of the USS BOXER. Like the CH-46 helo, the Sea Stallion flies in support of amphibious operations. Both types are capable of performing other tasks, including artillery lift, search and rescue, support of forward refueling and rearming points, and recovery of aircraft.* ABOVE: *The Commanding Officer of the amphibious assault ship the USS INCHON remains on the bridge while the ship conducts helicopter flight operations during GOMEX '97.*

Surface MCM is conducted by two new classes of ships. The AVENGER-class (MCM-1) minesweepers are 224 feet long, with a wooden hull and a crew of about 80. These ships are dual purpose, in that they have the ability to hunt mines or sweep them. They are equipped with mine-hunting sonar, and remotely piloted mine neutralization vehicles. They can also support embarked EOD Detachments, and have mine-sweeping equipment installed on the stern.

The smaller OSPREY-class (MHC-51) Coastal Mine Hunters are 184 feet long, with a reinforced fiberglass hull, and a crew of about 55. They carry the same sonar and mine neutralization vehicle as the MCM. The MHCs, however, do not deploy with embarked EOD detachments, and currently do not have a mine sweeping capability. Both classes of ships are extremely quiet and have a low magnetic signature which allows them to operate more safely in mine fields. These ships can be loaded on to a heavy sea-lift vessel for transport to the operations area, or travel under their own power. The strength of these ships lies in their sustainability and flexibility. When all three of the MCM forces are on scene together they function as a team, rapidly neutralizing the threat that mines present to the fleet. The surface forces can classify and identify contacts, and neutralize them. Air MCM can work with EOD, and combined they have a wide area search, identification and neutralization capability. Air and surface can even work in the same area, with air performing one type of sweep and surface either sweeping or hunting.

Another recent addition to the mine warfare community, USS INCHON (MCS 12), has improved the ability of the MCM squadron commanders to lead their forces. Converted from an amphibious assault ship to a mine countermeasures command, control and support vessel, Inchon can carry up to 30 helicopters, refuel and resupply both MHCs and MCMs, and support all aspects of the EOD mission. A flagship of the mine warfare fleet, Inchon will continue to serve into the next century. All of these MCM forces are deployed

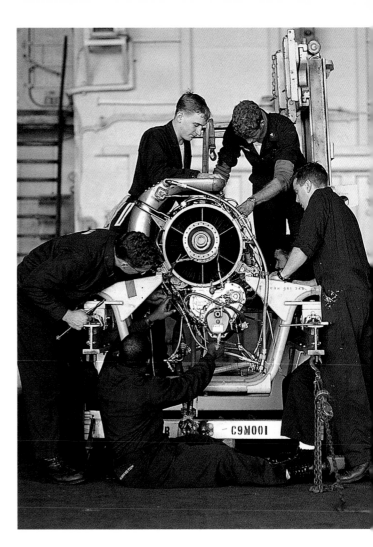

OPPOSITE, TOP LEFT & BOTTOM: *Helicopters on board the USS BOXER.* OPPOSITE, TOP RIGHT: *Aviation mechanics on board the USS INCHON have a reputation for making speedy repairs and turning around refurbished engines in record time.* ABOVE: *A CH-46 Sea Knight helicopter pilot waiting to launch from the USS INCHON.* RIGHT: *A Marine security watchstander keeps an ever-vigilant eye on the horizon.*

under the tactical control of the three Mine Counter-measures Squadrons (MCMRON), small staffs commanded by a captain. MCMRON One deals primarily with deployments and operations in the Pacific theater. MCMRON Two is responsible for the Atlantic theater, and MCMRON Three is responsible for supporting the U.S. Navy's Fifth Fleet in the Arabian Gulf. These squadrons plan operations and tactics used by the MCM Triad during exercises and coordinate operations with other nations.

The Squadron Commanders develop mine countermeasures plans based on the threat. The Squadrons work with theater or Task Force commanders to establish the goals of the MCM effort. The squadron commander then decides which forces in the triad can best accomplish his goals.

PRECEDING PAGES: *A Marine Harrier and a CH-53 Sea Stallion helicopter paint a dramatic silhouette on the deck of the USS BOXER.*
OPPOSITE, TOP LEFT: *During the Gulf War, the importance of military sealift was reaffirmed, represented here by an LST cramped with equipment.*
OPPOSITE, TOP RIGHT: *Whether ashore or afloat, Marine PFT (physical fitness training) is part of the daily routine.*
OPPOSITE BOTTOM: *The boiler room on board the amphibious assault ship the USS BOXER.*
RIGHT: *The USS BOXER under way off the California coast. This amphibious assault ship is a potent weapon system with embarked Marines, helicopters, Harrier V/STOL jet aircraft and a Landing Craft Air Cushion (LCAC).*
BELOW: *The helicopter inventory on board the USS BOXER includes the UH-1 Huey, left, and CH-46 Sea Knights shown here in a line abreast ready to launch.*
OVERLEAF: *The Air Boss on board the USS BOXER watches intently as one of his Harriers approaches for a landing during GOMEX-97.*

Opposite top: *A Marine CH-53E Super Stallion prepares to launch at dawn. Capable of lifting 16 tons of external load, it is the heaviest lift helicopter in the U.S. inventory.* Opposite bottom: *The USS INCHON flight deck at night.* Top: *Often, a successful Marine amphibious assault employs helicopters, landing craft, and a tank landing ship. This ship can be "beached," but more often simply lowers its bow ramp onto a floating pontoon causeway in order to unload its cargo of tanks, vehicles and equipment.* Below: *Combat-ready Marines await their transportation ashore.*

Overleaf: *A Marine AH-1 Seacobra flies over snow-capped mountains of Norway. These helicopters are specialized gunships that evolved from the widely used Huey series. They are deployed aboard amphibious assault ships and are flown by the Marine Corps' utility and attack squadrons.*

Fear of the Unknown

"Every Marine that is involved in the most vulnerable part of any amphibious operation — the ship-to-shore movement — experiences that knot in the very pit of his stomach as he boards the vehicle that will transport him from the ship to the shore. He thanks God for the professionalism of his brothers in arms, the men who wear the "blue" of that famous Navy-Marine Corps Team. It is they who serve in the "Gator Navy" that provide the security of a safe transport to the battle area, and they who are skilled coxswains who will get them safely to the shoreline. He even regrets, somewhat, some of the unkind remarks he made about the Sailors while in transit, but who he now appreciates so very much. He is also thankful for those Sailors who wear green uniforms, just like him, who are trained and prepared to perform life-saving actions on him and his fellow Marines, should they become injured by the enemy. He remembers the past heroic deeds of these corpsmen and is proud of the "special relationship" that has always existed between Marines and their corpsmen.

Yet in spite of these reassuring thoughts, he feels the sensation of absolute fear, as he steps off of the last rung of the rope ladder into the landing craft. On that long ride from ship-to-shore, he ponders unanswerable questions: Is the beach defended? How heavily? Did the naval gunfire prep fires do their job? Is the landing zone "hot?" Will we even reach

BELOW: *The wait is over — Marines walk up the rear ramp of a CH-46 Sea Knight for transportation to the beach.* OPPOSITE TOP: *In the welldeck of the USS BOXER a discussion of the final plans for an amphibious assault. Loaded LCACs are ready to exit the back of the ship. LCACs have twin, four-blade aircraft propellers and two maneuverable gas turbine exhausts.* OPPOSITE, BOTTOM: *Sometimes the wait can seem interminable.*

the beach? Did the EOD and SEAL teams remove the underwater obstacles? And more. Most of all, however, he is fearful that he will let his fellow Marines down when the going gets tough. He knows that he is well trained, as are all on his landing craft, but when faced with the ferocity of bullets, mortars, artillery, air strikes, and the yelling and confusion that accompanies an opposed amphibious landing against a determined enemy, he is always unsure of how he will react. He doesn't know that everyone in the landing craft is having the identical conversation with themselves. It is this fear, the fear of the unknown — of so many unknowns, that generates the adrenalin in the blood stream of Marines that ultimately elicits the judgement, "Uncommon Valor was a Common Virtue."

Marines in the years gone by would find it hard to conceive of an LCAC vehicle that moved them at great speed from ships that were "beyond the horizon" to perhaps less well defended beaches. I doubt, however, that today's Marine will have any less of a knot in his stomach as the craft proceeds; just less time to ponder this uncomfortable feeling as the LCAC closes at what he might consider "breakneck speed." Now he is thankful for the commitment, research and development by military and civilians that have contributed to reducing his vulnerability during this most critical phase in an amphibious operation."

— Fritz Warren is a former assistant operations officer with Special Landing Force "Alpha" off the coast of Vietnam during 1967; and operations officer for Battalion Landing Team 2/4 in northern "I Corps" in country during 1968. He is a survivor of the Battle of Dai Do April 20-May 2, 1968.

OPPOSITE, TOP AND BOTTOM: *The USS NASSAU steams off the coast of Norway. Weather can play a significant role in exercises. The flight deck must be clear of snow and ice before flight operations may commence. TOP: A Marine Harrier lifts off.*

PRECEDING PAGES: *Fire protective clothing can be put to other uses. This Sailor leans into the wind but remains dry as he crosses the flight deck during a rain squall on board the USS NASSAU off the coast of Norway.*

OPPOSITE TOP: *An LCAC delivers Marine equipment ashore.*

OPPOSITE BOTTOM: *The control compartment of an LCAC resembles the cockpit of an aircraft. With excellent visibility on three sides, the operator sits on the right, the engineer in the center, and the navigator sits on the left. LCACs can clear land obstacles to four feet and are designed with a payload of 60 tons — capable of carrying one M1 Abrams tank or four Light Armored Vehicles (LAVs).*

BELOW: *An LCAC in eastern Australia has just left the rear well deck of the USS ESSEX (LHD-2). The advantages of landing craft air cushions are numerous. They can carry heavy payloads such as the M-1 tank at speeds approaching 46 miles per hour. Their payload and speed means more forces reach the beach faster, with shorter intervals between trips. The air cushion allows this vehicle to reach 70 percent of the world's coastline. Just 87 feet long with a beam of 47 feet, and a crew of five, LCACs displace 151 tons when loaded.*

OVERLEAF: *A member of the Navy's Beach Detachment directs LCACs on a beach in the Caribbean.*

LEFT: *A helicopter prepares to land in Norway during cold weather training exercises.*

BELOW: *A Marine M-1 tank prepares to leave an LCAC on a California beach. Mild temperatures and proximity to West Coast Navy and Marine Corps bases make California an attractive site for year-round training exercises.*

OPPOSITE: *A Marine CH-53E Super Stallion departs the rugged terrain of Norway with weapons for the fleet during cold weather training exercises.*

OVERLEAF: *Marines display their flexibility and versatility by coming ashore from an Amphibian Assault Vehicle (AAV) during cold weather training in Norway. The mission of the AAV is to transport troops and equipment through rough waters and the surf zone to inland objectives and subsequent tactical operations. With a crew of five, the AAV can transport 18 combat troops, and it has a cargo capacity of nearly 9,000 pounds. It can travel 7 miles per hour in the water and 45 miles per hour on land. The AAV is equipped with smoke grenade launchers and a .50 caliber machine gun.*

ABOVE: *Members of a SEAL Team attach a Limpet mine to the hull of a surface vessel. Through powerful suction, Limpet mines quickly and easily attach to any smooth or shiny non-porous surface.*

OPPOSITE TOP: *SEALs rappel to the ground from an Army UH-60 Black Hawk helicopter during training in Panama.*

OPPOSITE BOTTOM: *Marines and Seabees set up base camp during cold weather training in Norway.*

OVERLEAF: *During training exercises in California, these Marines apprehend and "secure" a prisoner of war.*

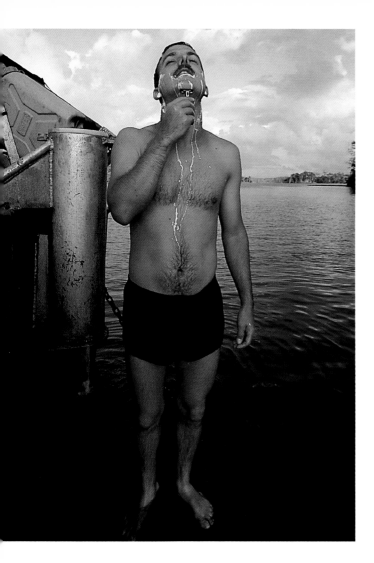

PRECEDING PAGES: *SEALs travel quietly and covertly and can arrive from the sea leaving no footprints. These self-sufficient warriors conduct clandestine operations behind enemy lines.*

OPPOSITE: *These SEALs are capable of living for weeks without support. Superb crack shots, they receive training with weapons at Quantico, Virginia.*

LEFT: *An SBU (Special Boat Unit) crewman shaves "on maneuvers" without the aid of a mirror.*

BELOW: *A SEAL communicates from an ice cave during training exercises in Norway.*

Naval special forces, the UDTs (Underwater Demolition Teams) and even more extensively trained SEAL (Sea-Air-Land) Teams bring unique, specialized skills to the Naval Service. Both UDTs and SEALs can be "delivered" by helicopter or fixed-wing aircraft, via surface ships, or even submarines. They may be employed as saboteurs, planting explosives or detonating maritime structures; special agents; as snipers; intelligence gathering and more.

BOTTOM: *SEALs march in Alaskan snowdrifts. They wear dark sunglasses to protect their eyes from the bright sunlight reflected off the snow.*

OPPOSITE TOP: *In Australia during Tandem Thrust '97, these Marines conducting ground maneuvers were some of more than 21,500 U.S. personnel participating in the month-long training exercise. Australia participated in the exercise for the first time in 1997.*

OPPOSITE BELOW: *Marine snipers wearing Ghillies suits for good camouflage can remain absolutely still for hours on end, seemingly oblivious to personal discomfort.*

OVERLEAF: *A SEAL rifleman trains in Panama.*

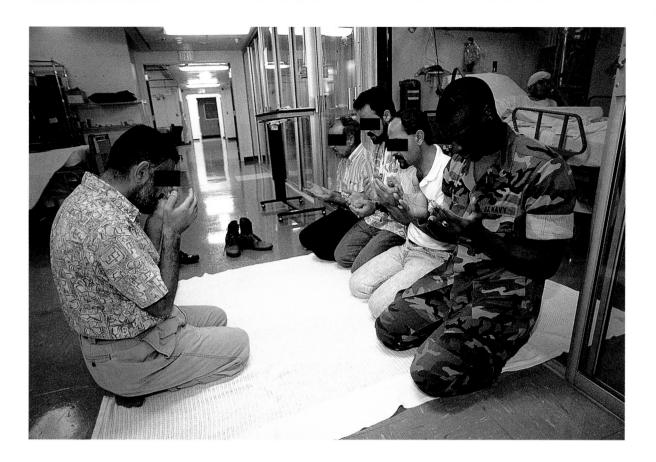

Building Bridges; Building Lives then . . .

OPPOSITE: *Seabee capabilities include: construction engineering; horizontal, vertical, utility, and underwater construction; and support skill in areas as diverse as mechanical and medical engineering. Here, using natural raw materials, Seabees construct a bridge in Australia.* ABOVE: *A Seabee inspects a floating dock on Guam.* TOP: *The U.S. Navy's first Moslem chaplain prays with Kurds evacuated from Iraq and seeking refuge and asylum on Guam.*

OPPOSITE: *U.S. Air Force Master Sergeant Joe Sitterly communicates with an AN/PRC-112 survival radio during Search and rescue (SAR) training exercises at Shoalwater Bay Training Area, Queensland, Australia. This new radio is the same one Air Force Captain Scott O'Grady had in his possession when he was shot down over Bosnia. The radio assisted the search and rescue efforts with its new, high-tech capabilities which include deterring the enemy from directionally finding a downed pilot.*

RIGHT: *A Tandem Thrust '97 exercise participant prepares for recovery by studying an evasion chart and communicating his location to the rescue task force.*

Inter-Service Cooperation

"During Exercise Tandem Thrust, in Australia this spring, I directed all Combat Search and rescue (CSAR) scenarios as the senior control group CSAR controller. Most of the events involved U.S. Navy forces from the command ship the USS BLUE RIDGE (LCC-19) and the aircraft carrier the USS INDEPENDENCE. Because events involved simulated shoot-downs of U.S. Navy aircraft in low to medium threat hostile environments, successful recovery of downed aviators required many activities — including report of the shoot-down; location and authentication of evaders; forming a combat search and rescue task force to maximize both recovery and survivability.

Navy air crews who volunteered to play survivors and evaders linked up with me two days before their scheduled CSAR events to brush up on concealment, navigation, signaling, and communications skills. The evader is the weak link during CSAR missions. During exercises, participants who cannot perform basic evasion and recovery (E & R) skills, are a liability. During past conflicts those who neglected to prepare for evasion very often hampered the recovery process and/or became prisoners of war."

— Master Sergeant Sitterly is a career U.S. Air Force Survival Instructor, and the Evasion and Recovery Program Manager assigned to the Pacific Rescue Coordination Center at Hickam Air Force Base, Hawaii.

ABOVE AND OPPOSITE: *A SEAL Special Boat Unit training in Panama. Their boats have low radar signatures and quiet, powerful engines, well-suited for clandestine operations.*

OVERLEAF: *An Amphibian Assault Vehicle (AAV) comes ashore during training exercises in Norway.*

LEFT: *A trained rifleman, this member of a Special Boat Unit keeps an ever-vigilant eye, scanning the horizon for movement.*

BELOW: *During riverine operations in Central America, Special Boat Unit crewmen spend weeks at a time subsisting on the environment. A simple hammock is their preferred bed, but protecting their patrol craft means their rest comes from only cat naps.*

OPPOSITE: *Members of a SEAL team review a map while planning their next maneuver with Army pilots in Panama.*

OPPOSITE: *Special Boat Unit crewmen clean their weapons on the deck of their Mark III 65-foot patrol boat.*

RIGHT: *Hospital Corpsman Second Class Michael Broschart examines a snake for identification during Operation Tandem Thrust in Australia. His work is critically important since six of the world's ten most deadly snakes inhabit Shoalwater Bay Training Areas in Queensland, Australia, site for much of the land-phase of this exercise.*

BELOW: *During peace-time training exercises, as in battle, the environment can be a dangerous enemy. Our Navy has the capability of deploying a Public Health Laboratory to almost anywhere in the world, and the responsibility and obligation to protect the safety and health of those serving in our Armed Forces. During Tandem Thrust '97 in Australia, the deployed Public Health Laboratory staff collected and studied more than 100,000 mosquitoes. These insects can spread many viruses that cause human illness. Shown here, Lieutenant Commander Stanton Cope, Medical Service Corps, U.S. Navy, processes mosquitoes for viruses. His goal was to prevent illness in exercise participants and to identify any new viruses that were present in Australia.*

"A dolphin's life expectancy outside the Navy is about 18 years. We have a number of dolphins that are 30 years old or older. The reason is simple: Dolphins in the Navy have complete veterinarian care — quarterly exams; complete annual physicals; antibiotics when they are sick; vitamins to supplement their diet; a very controlled diet and caloric intake. Our dolphins are pampered. They love it here!"

— Lieutenant Commander Adam Guziewicz
Executive Officer, Explosive Ordnance
Detachment (EOD) Mobile Unit Three

PRECEDING PAGES: *Framed by a setting sun in southern California, this Bottlenose dolphin is playing behind the 22-foot Boston Whaler used to transport her to the exercise area.* LEFT AND RIGHT: *A dolphin is rewarded with a fish after completing an exercise.* OPPOSITE BOTTOM: *A veterinarian is assigned to EOD Mobile Unit Three to ensure the dolphins, like this one aboard a Boston Whaler, remain in good health.* BELOW: *Part of their good health routine is a daily tooth brushing to prevent gingivitis.*

Dolphins Contribute to the Navy's Mine Countermeasures Effort

With names like Luke, Fathom, Jake, Splash, Dinky and Cookie, the Navy's marine mammals are an integral part of our mine countermeasures capabilities. They are used for mine detection and neutralization, swimmer defense, and in the recovery of exercise mines and torpedoes.

As Lieutenant Commander Adam Guziewicz, Executive Officer of Explosive Ordnance Detachment, Mobile Unit Three, based in San Diego, told me, "Dolphins are a simply fantastic asset. It is a case of technology not catching up with nature. We simply can't compete with a dolphin's bio sonar. Dolphins are the most capable, cost effective and efficient resource available for mine hunting and neutralization." In some situations the mammals are much more effective than people or existing hardware.

The fleet's operational marine mammal system detachments, comprising about 40 animals, are assigned to EOD Mobile Units at San Diego (dolphins and sea lions) and Charleston (sea lions). Dolphins detect and neutralize buoyant, close-tethered mines moored near the bottom which makes them more difficult to detect and identify. They also detect, locate, and mark or neutralize mines on the ocean's floor, and even those buried below the bottom.

Dolphins provide defense for harbors, anchorages, and individual ships against swimmers and divers. First used at Cam Rahn Bay in Vietnam, these dolphins participate regularly in fleet exercises and real-world base security. They were deployed to Bahrain during Operation Earnest Will in 1988. During 1994, a Third Fleet exercise, RIMPAC 94, successfully operated a variety of dolphin systems. Some made the 11-day surface transit aboard the USS JUNEAU (LPD-10); the remainder flew directly to Pearl Harbor from San Diego aboard strategic airlift aircraft.

When used to neutralize mines, the dolphin and sea lions carry a package with a timer on it. They are trained to deposit the package in the proximity of the mine before turning away and swimming out of danger before the explosive is detonated. The dolphins are smart, and are fast swimmers.

Explosive Ordnance Disposal (EOD)

Whether it's some 1,300 naval mines in the northern Persian Gulf that frustrated U.S. plans for an amphibious assault to liberate Kuwait during Operation desert Storm, . . . more than 100 million land mines "leftover" from wars in 62 countries . . . an armed bomb "hung up" on an aircraft aboard an aircraft carrier . . . or a terrorist's improvised explosive device that threatens a U.S. embassy, unexploded ordnance poses grave risks for military forces and civilians alike. This modern crisis must be dealt with professionally by trained experts.

ABOVE: *Members of an EOD team stationed at Guam continue to search for and clear unexploded ordnance left from World War II. These Sailors are inside a 15-foot crater left by an exploded bomb.*

RIGHT: *EOD divers learn the importance of approaching objects on the ocean floor with caution. Step one is identification which must come before rendering devices safe and recovering them for analysis.*

OPPOSITE: *EOD divers attach an explosive package to neutralize a floating mine (TOP), and a tethered mine in the Pacific Ocean off the coast of Hawaii.*

The job of "rendering safe" unexploded ordnance of whatever origin or age is the responsibility of an elite group of specialists: Explosive Ordnance Disposal (EOD) Teams. While all branches of the U.S. Armed Forces employ EOD people, only the United States Navy EOD force of 1,000 men and women has the equipment, extensive training and mobility to deal effectively and swiftly with the global spectrum of threats — from conventional ordnance to nuclear, chemical, and biological weapons. Trained as explosive ordnance disposal technicians, divers, demolition experts, and even parachutists, these professionals have the awesome responsibility of protecting the people, ships, aircraft, and installations, whenever and wherever they may be in jeopardy from unexploded ordnance.

The biggest difference between the EOD divers in the Mine Warfare community and Navy UDTs and SEALs is their mission. SEAL Teams are considered an offensive force; EOD Teams exist as a support force to protect life and property. The two groups occasionally work together. During the Gulf War, for example, EOD Teams were sent to ensure the oil rig platforms used as bases for Iraqi military operations weren't booby-trapped so the SEALs could destroy them in safety.

When the multi-national coalition that defeated Saddam Hussein turned its attention to Operation Provide Comfort to help Kurdish refugees in northern Iraq, extensive munitions caches and land mines hindered humanitarian efforts. Two EOD terchnicians from the USS THEODORE ROOSEVELT and two Marine Corps EOD technicians destroyed 20,000 ordnance items with a collective weight of more than 33 tons.

Navy EOD conducts diving and search operations in support of the Coast Guard, Treasury, Secret Service, and U. S. Customs Service in counter-narcotics and drug interdiction efforts. In the aftermath of the 1993 World Trade Center Bombing, they provided assistance to the FBI; and EOD divers contributed to the efforts in raising TWA Flight 800 off Long Island in 1996.

As U.S. forces continue to move from the sea into the littorals, members of the Navy EOD community will help clear the way.

OPPOSITE: *On board a buoy in the Pacific Ocean off the island of Guam, an EOD technician raises his right hand to reenlist for four more years of service in the United States Navy.* BELOW: *To celebrate, he and his fellow EOD teammates take a dip in the ocean.*

TRAINING
The Key to Readiness

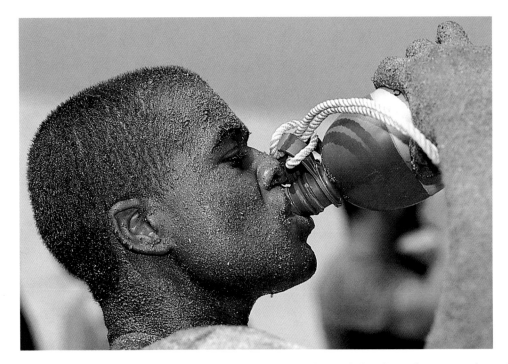

PRECEDING PAGES: *BUDS (Basic Underwater Demolition School) students run along the southern California beaches. Physical fitness training is an integral part of every Marine's day.*

ON THESE PAGES: *Many say that BUDS training is the most physically and mentally challenging the Navy has to offer. With a 70 percent attrition rate, they must be right. Beginning with eight weeks of physical conditioning, the second phase of training involves more physical conditioning and adds seven weeks of scuba diving. The third phase is the longest (10 weeks) and concentrates on land warfare, weapons handling and explosive ordnance. If a student successfully completes all three phases, he earns the privilege of trying to become a SEAL.*

Whether it is enlisted Boot Camp at Great Lakes, Illinois or Orlando, Florida, the United States Naval Academy, formal Navy Schools, or on the job — it all adds up to training. It starts out slow and easy and gets progressively more difficult. But it's obvious why training is critically important. Today's ships, aircraft, and weapons systems are designed to take advantage of state of the art technology. With that as a backdrop, it's easy to understand why 99% of our new accessions have a high school diploma, and why most go on to receive advanced training, many even before they arrive at their first duty station.

LEFT: *At Boot Camp in Orlando, recruits spend a lot of time learning military customs and traditions, including the fine art of marching.*

BELOW: *Marching under Florida's hot sun can be dehydrating, so canteens are issued to all recruits. This water break could be the first breather since breakfast.*

OPPOSITE: *A Chief Petty Officer instructor illustrates some of the finer points of communicating with semaphore flags. This student has completed recruit training and is now studying to become a Signalman.*

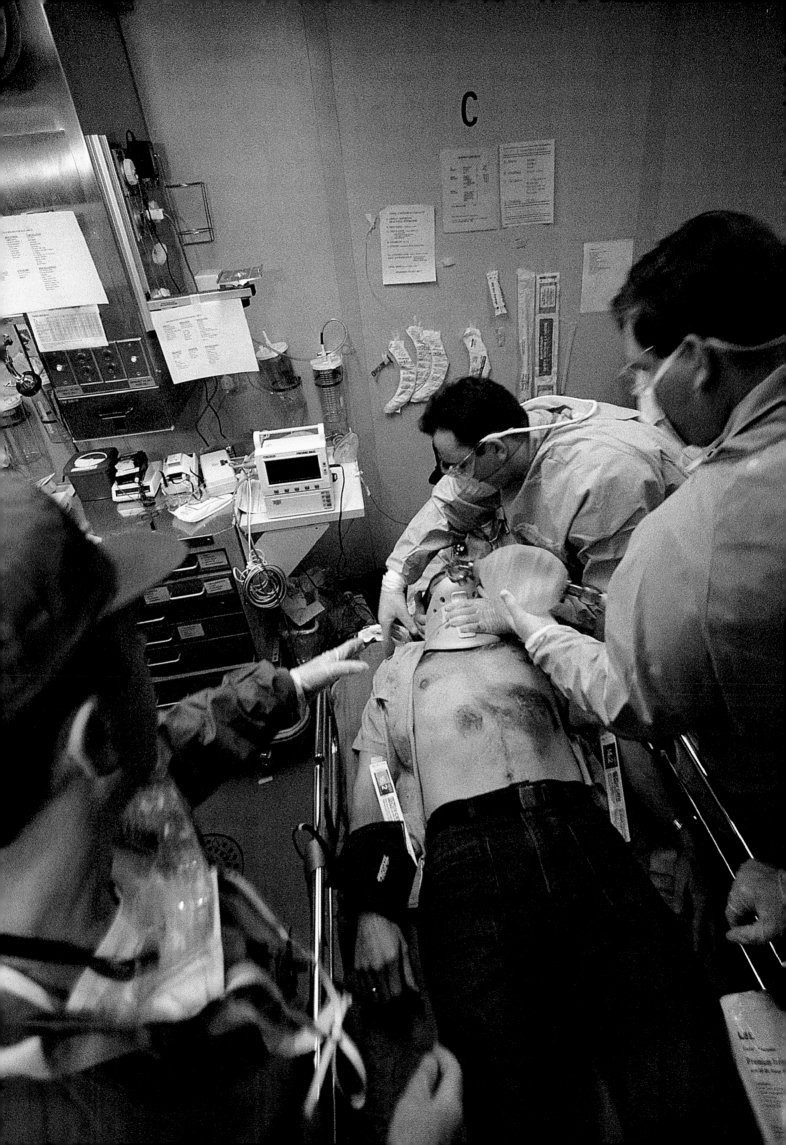

OPPOSITE: *Medical personnel receive valuable training on board the hospital ship USNS MERCY (TAH-19). With a crew comprised of active duty and reserve personnel, this ship, and her "sister," the USNS COMFORT (TAH-20) are former commercial tankers that have been converted into floating hospitals, complete with 12 operating rooms, four X-ray rooms, a blood bank, pharmacy, an intensive care unit capable of handling 80 patients, plus nearly a thousand additional beds. With a helicopter landing deck, they can accept medevac casualties. These two ships are designed to support the deployment of American personnel deployed overseas in combat operations.*

ABOVE: *Scale model ships like the KNOX — class frigate and the SPRUANCE — class destroyer were considered excellent surface ship platforms for training junior officers to Captains back in the 1970s. Here, young surface warfare warriors could see the response time to engine and helm orders, and learn the fine art of shiphandling, without suffering the costly consequences of a ship collision. Thucydides is credited with the saying, "A collision at sea can ruin your entire day." In today's Navy, a collision at sea ruins far more than a commanding officer's day — it usually terminates his career. These model boats have been replaced by virtual reality simulators.*

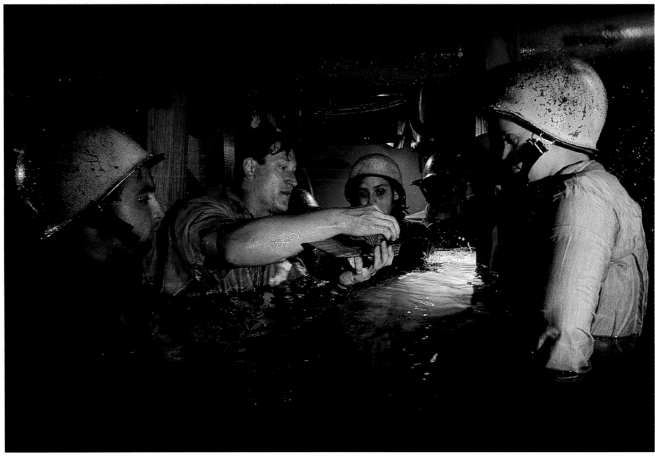

TOP AND OPPOSITE: *Nothing is more frightening or dangerous than a fire at sea, but detecting them is easier — even behind bulkheads — with infrared thermal imaging devices. As a result, Navy firefighters suffer less from heat, smoke, and toxic fumes. Quick response and conquering one's fear are the keys to efficiently extinguishing a blaze.* ABOVE: *At the Navy's Damage Control School in Newport, Rhode Island, countless sailors have learned the finer points of saving a sinking ship in the trainer the USS BUTTERCUP. Shown here, a damage control instructor discusses the correct way to patch a leak to minimize flooding in a shipboard compartment.*

TOP LEFT: *A young helmsman on a tugboat receives valuable on-the-job training. Even though he's not looking right at her, you can sense the tugboat captain is observing her every move.*

LEFT AND ABOVE: *Sniper school at Quantico, Virginia*

ABOVE: *In New London, Connecticut, they take training seriously at Naval Submarine School. Instructors of damage control training sit at sophisticated simulators, observing students in action.*

RIGHT: *Flooding aboard a submarine can present even more serious problems for a crew than in a surface ship. This damage control trainer simulates the general arrangement of the forward end of the lower level engine-room of a ballistic missile submarine. Here students learn first hand how to apply damage control procedures. This compartment can flood with more than 20,000 gallons of cold water at a rate of 1200 gallons per minute.*

ABOVE AND BELOW: *After completing Plebe year at the United States Naval Academy, students carry out a tradition — whoever can replace the hat taped at the peak of the greased Herndon Monument with his or her own cover will be the first member of the graduating class promoted to admiral.*

OPPOSITE: *A sky alive with hats, these midshipmen celebrate the end of four years of dedicated study and discipline.*

TECHNICAL APPENDICES

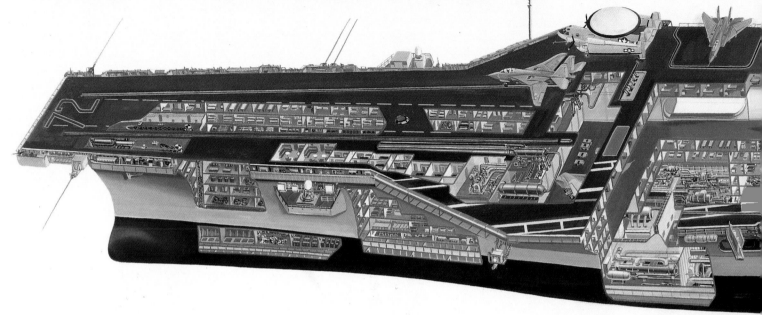

ABOVE: *The U.S.S. ABRAHAM LINCOLN (CVN-72) was commissioned in November 1989. A NIMITZ-class aircraft carrier, this ship is powered by two Westinghouse nuclear reactors that power four steam turbines and propellers. Capable of speeds exceeding 35 miles per hour, the ship is longer than 3.5 football fields, and its flight deck is 257 feet wide, encompassing 4.5 acres. With an embarked air wing of approximately 80 aircraft, the USS ABRAHAM LINCOLN is manned by 5,500 people.*

RIGHT: *The U.S.S. NIMITZ (CVN-68) joined the fleet on May 3, 1975.*

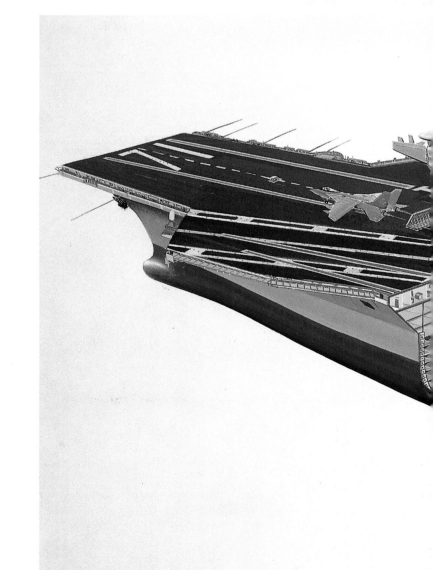

A-6E INTRUDER
MEDIUM ATTACK AIRCRAFT

Service: Navy and Marine Corps

Description: The A-6E Intruder is a carrier-based medium attack bomber.

Mission: The A-6E was developed for conventional ground attack in all weather conditions, day and night.

Features: The A-6E is an all-weather, two-seat, subsonic, carrier-based attack aircraft. In spite of its weight, it has excellent slow-flying capabilities with full span slats and flaps. The crew, sitting side by side, can see in all directions through a broad canopy. The aircraft is equipped with a micro-miniaturized digital computer, a solid state weapons release system, and a single integrated track and search radar. The Intruder is armed with laser-guided weapons and equipped with a chin turret containing a forward-looking infra-red (FLIR) system and laser designator and receiver.

The A-6 worked around the clock in Vietnam, conducting attacks on the targets with a pinpoint accuracy unavailable through any other aircraft at that time. The A-6E proved once again that it is the best all-weather precision bomber in the world in the joint strike on Libyan terrorist-related targets in 1986. Navy A-6E Intruders and Air Force FB-111s penetrated the sophisticated Libyan air defense systems which had been alerted by the high level of diplomatic tension and by rumors of impending attacks. Evading more than 100 guided missiles, the strike force flew at low altitudes in complete darkness and hit its target. A-6 aircraft were used extensively during Operation Desert Storm, providing precision bombing on a wide range of targets. The night and all-weather attack capabilities enabled the A-6 to neutralize anti-aircraft batteries and attack well-protected tactical targets with minimum casualties. The precision munitions used by the A-6 provided exact targeting of targets in a complex environment.

GENERAL CHARACTERISTICS

Primary Function: All-weather medium attack aircraft

Contractor: Grumman Aerospace Corporation

Unit Cost: $22 million

Propulsion: Two Pratt & Whitney J52-P8B engines (9300 pounds/4185 kg thrust each)

Wingspan: 53 feet 7 inches (16.1 meters)

Length: 54 feet 7 inches (16.1 meters)

Height: 16 feet 3 inches (4.95 meters)

Weight: Take-off maximum gross, 60,626 pounds (27,524 kg); take-off maximum gross (carrier), 58,600 pounds (26,370 kg); empty, 25,630 pounds (11,636 kg)

Speed: 563 knots (648 miles, 1036 km, per hour)

Ceiling: 44,600 feet

Range: With full combat load, 1,077 miles (1,733 km); with external fuel tanks, 3,100 miles (4,991 km)

Armament: Five stores locations each rated at 3,600 pounds (1,634 kg) carrying any combination of Mk 80 series GP bombs, Guided Bomb Units (GBUs), AGM-65 Maverick missiles, AGM-88 Harm missiles, AGM-84D Harpoon missiles, AIM-9 Sidewinder missiles, and the AGM-62 Walleye.

Crew: Two

Date Deployed: First flight, April 19, 1960; Operational, February 1963

C-2A GREYHOUND

Service: Navy and Marine Corps

Description: Twin-engine cargo aircraft designed to land on aircraft carriers.

Features: The C-2A Greyhound provides critical logistics support to aircraft carriers. It's primary mission is carrier on-board delivery, Powered by two T-46 turboprop engines, the C-2A can deliver a payload of up to 10,000 pounds. The cabin can readily accommodate cargo, passengers, or both. It is also equipped to accept litter patients in medical evacuation missions.

Priority cargo such as jet engines can be transported from shore to ship in a matter of hours. A cage system or transport stand provides cargo restraint for loads during carrier launch or landing. The large aft cargo ramp and door and a powered winch allow straight-in rear cargo loading and downloading for fast turnaround.

The C-2A's open-ramp flight capability allows airdrop of supplies and personnel from a carrier-launched aircraft. This, plus its folding wings and an on-board auxiliary power unit for engine starting and ground power self-sufficiency in remote areas provide an operational versatility found in no other cargo aircraft.

Background: The original C-2A aircraft were overhauled, and their operational life extended, in 1973. In 1984, a contract was awarded for 39 new C-2A aircraft to replace earlier airframes. Dubbed the Reprocured C-2A due to the similarity to the original, the new aircraft include substantial improvements in airframe and avionic systems. All the older C-2As were phased out in 1987, and the last of the new models was delivered in 1990. During the period November 1985 to February 1987, VR-24, operating with seven Reprocured C-2As, demonstrated exceptional operational readiness while delivering two million pounds of cargo, two million pounds of mail, and 14,000 passengers in spport of the European and Mediterranean theatres.

GENERAL CHARACTERISTICS

Primary Function: Carrier-on-board delivery (COD) aircraft

Contractor: Grumman Aerospace Corporation

Unit Cost: $38.96 million

Propulsion: Two Allison T-56-A-425 turboprop engines; 4,600 shaft horsepower each

Length: 57 feet 7 inches (17.3 meters)

Height: 17 feet (5 meters)

Weight: Max, gross, take-off: 57,000 pounds (25,650 kg)

Cruising Speed: Max.: 300 knots (345 miles per hour, 553 km per hour)

Ceiling: 30,000 feet (9,100 meters)

Range: 1,300 nautical mils (1,495 statute miles)

Crew: Four

C-130 HERCULES

Service: Navy, Marine Corps, Air Force, Coast Guard

Description: The C-130 Hercules, a four-engine turboprop aircraft, affectionately known world-wide as "Herky", is the workhorse of the military services. Capable of landing and taking off from short, rough dirt runways, it is a people and cargo hauler and is used in a wide variety of other roles, such as gunships, weather watchers, tankers, firefighters and aerial ambulances. There are more than 40 versions of the Hercules and it is widely used by more than 50 nations.

Two Navy LC-130 "Herkys" are assigned to the National Science Foundation, equipped with skis as wel as wheels for operations in support of scientific research in Antarctica.

Background: Deliveries of the C-130A to the U.S. military began in December 1956 and the first B models came on board in April 1959. The newest is the H model.

GENERAL CHARACTERISTICS

Primary Function: Global airlift

Contractor: Lockheed Aeronautical Systems Company, Marietta, Ga.

Power Plant: Four Allison T56-A-15 turbo-props, each 4,300 horsepower

Thrust: Horsepower each engine: AC-130A, 3,750 hp; AC-130H, 4,910 hp

Length: 97 feet 9 inches (29.3 meters)

Height: 38 feet 3 inches (11.4 meters)

Wingspan: 132 feet 7 inches (39.7 meters)

Speed: 374 mph (Mach 0.57, 604.4 kmh) at 20,000 feet

Ceiling: 33,000 feet with 100,000 pounds (45,000 kg) payload

Maximum Takeoff Weight: 155,000 pounds (69,750 kg)

Range: 2,350 miles (2,050 nautical miles, 3,770 km) with maximum payload; 2,500 miles (2,174 nautical miles, 4,000 km) with 25,000

pounds (11,259kg) cargo; 5,200 miles (4,522 nautical miles, 8,320 km) with no cargo

Unit Cost: Average $44.1 million

Crew: Five: two pilots, navigator, flight engineer, loadmaster

Capacity: Up to 92 troops or 64 paratroops or 74 litter patients or five standard freight pallets

E-2C HAWKEYE

Description: The E-2C Hawkeye is the Navy's all-weather, carrier-based tactical warning and control system aircraft.

Features: The Hawkeye provides all-weather airborne early warning and command and control functions for the carrier battle group. Additional missions include surface surveillance coordination, strike and interceptor control, search and rescue guidance and communications relay. An integral component of the carrier air wing, the E-2C uses computerized sensors to provide early warning, threat analyses and control of counteraction against air and surface targets.

Background: Carrier-based E-2C Hawkeyes directed F-14 Tomcat fighters flying combat air patrol during two-carrier battle group joint strike against terrorist-related Libyan targets in 1986. E-2Cs and AEGIS cruisers working together, provided total air mass superiority over the American fleet.

More recently, E-2Cs provided the command and control for successful operations during the Persian Gulf War, directing both land attack and combat air patrol missions over Iaq and providing control for the shoot-down of two Iraqi MIG-21 aircraft by carrier-based F/A-18s in the early days of the war.

E-2 aircraft also have worked extremely effectively with U.S. law enforcement agencies in drug interdiction operations.

E-2C aircraft entered U.S. Navy service with Airborne Early Warning Squadron 123 at Naval Air Station norfolk, Va. In November 1973.

GENERAL CHARACTERISTICS

Primary Function: Airborne early warning, command and control

Contractor: Grumman Aerospace Corp.

Unit Cost: $51 million

Propulsion: Two Allison T-56-A427 turboprop engines; (5,000 shaft horsepower each)

Length: 57 feet 6 inches (17.5 meters)

Height: 18 feet 3 inches (5.6 meters)

Wingspan: 80 feet 7 inches (28 meters)

Weight: Max. gross take-off: 53,000 lbs (23,850 kg) 40,200 lbs basic (18,090 kg)

Speed: 300+ knots (345 miles, 552 km. Per hour)

Ceiling: 30,000 feet (9,100 meters)

Crew: Five

Armament: None

Date Deployed: First flight: October 1960; Operational: January 1964

E-6A TACAMO

Description: Provides secure, survivable jam-resistant strategic communications relay for fleet ballistic submarines

Background: Boeing derived this aircraft from its commercial 707 to replace the aging EC-130Q and perform the Navy's TACAMO ("Take Charge and Move Out") mission of linking ballistic missile forces with national command authority during time of crisis. The aircraft carries a low frequency communication system and wire antenna several thousand feet long that is winched in and out of the aircraft. The first E-6 was accepted by the Navy in August 1989.

GENERAL CHARACTERISTICS

Primary Function: Airborne command post for fleet ballistic missile submarines

Contractor: Boeing

Unit Cost: $141.7 million

Propulsion: Four CFM-56-2A-2 High bypass turbofans

Length: 150 feet 4 inches (45.8 meters)

Height: 42 feet 5 inches (12.9 meters)

Wingspan: 148 feet 4 inches (45.2 meters)

Weight: Max gross take-off: 341,000 pounds (153,900 kg)

Ceiling: Above 40,000 feet

Speed: 522 knots, 600 miles (960 km) per hour

Crew: 14

Range: 6,600 nautical miles (7,590 statute miles, 12,144 km) with 6 hours loiter time

Armament: None

EA-6B PROWLER

Service: Navy and Marine Corps

Description: The EA-6B Prowler provides an umbrella of protection over strike aircraft and ships by jamming enemy radar, electronic data links and communication.

Features: The EA-6B Prowler is a twin-engine, mid-wing aircraft manufactured by Grumman Aerospace Corporation as a modification of the basic A-6 Intruder airframe. Designed for carrier and advanced base operations, the Prowler is a fully integrated electronic warfare system combining long-range, all-weather capabilities with advanced electronic countermeasures. A forward equipment bay, and pod-shaped faring on the vertical fin, house the additional avionics equipment. The side-by-side cockpit arrangement gives maximum efficiency, visibility and comfort.

Background: The primary mission of the aircraft is to support air strikes and ground troops by interrupting enemy electronics activity.

GENERAL CHARACTERISTICS

Primary Function: Electronic countermeasures

Contractor: Grumman Aerospace Corporation

Propulsion: Two Pratt & Whitney J52-P408 engines (11,200 pounds thrust each)

Length: 59 feet 10 inches (17.7 meters)

Wingspan: 53 feet (15.9 meters)

Height: 16 feet 3 inches (4.9 meters)

Weight: Max gross take-off: 61,000 pounds (27,450 kg)

Speed: Over 500 knots (575 mph, 920 kmh)

Range: Over 1,000 nautical miles (1,150 statute miles, 1,840 km)

Ceiling: 37,600 feet

Crew: Four: pilot and three electronic countermeasures officers

Armament: AGM-88A HARM missile

Date Deployed: First flight, May 25, 1968; Operational, July 1971

F-14 TOMCAT

Description: The F-14 Tomcat is a supersonic, twin-engine, variable sweep-wing, two-place fighter designed to attack and destroy enemy aircraft at night and in all weather conditions.

Features: The F-14 can track up to 24 targets simultaneously with its advanced weapons control system and attack six with Phoenix AIM-54A missiles while continuing to scan the airspace. Armament includes a mix of other air intercept missiles, rockets and bombs.

Background: The Grumman F-14, the world's premier air defense fighter, was designed to replace the F-4 Phantom II fighter (phased out in 1986). F-14s provided air cover for the joint strike on Libyan terrorist targets in 1986. The F-14A was introduced in the mid-1970s. The upgraded F-14A+ version, with new General Electric F-110 engines, now widespread throughout the fleet, is more than a match for enemy fighters in close-in, air combat.

GENERAL CHARACTERISTICS

Function: Carrier-based multi-role strike fighter

Contractor: Grumman Aerospace Corporation

Unit Cost: $38 million

Propulsion: F-14: two Pratt & Whitney TF-30P-414A turbofan engines with afterburners; F-14B and F-14D: two General Electric F-110-GE-400 augmented turbofan engines with afterburners

Thrust: F-14A: 20,900 pounds (9,405 kg) static thrust per engine; F-14B and F-14D: 27,000 pounds (12,150 kg) per engine

Length: 61 feet 9 inches (18.6 meters)

Height: 16 feet (4.8 meters)

Maximum Takeoff Weight: 72,900 pounds (32,805 kg)

Wingspan: 64 feet (19 meters) unswept; 38 feet (11.4 meters) swept

Ceiling: Above 50,000 feet

Speed: Mach 2+

Crew: Two: pilot and radar intercept officer

Armament: Up to 13,000 pounds of AIM-54 Phoenix missile, AIM-7 Sparrow missile, AIM-9 Sidewinder missile, air-to-ground ordnance, and one MK-61A1 Vulcan 20mm cannon

Date Deployed: First flight: December 1970

F/A-18 HORNET

Service: Navy and Marine Corps

Description: All-weather fighter and attack aircraft. The single-seat F/A-18 Hornet is the nation's first strike-fighter. It was designed for traditional strike applications such as interdiction and close air support without compromising its fighter capabilities. With its excellent fighter and self-defense capabilities, the F/A-18 at the same time increases strike mission survivability and supplements the F-14 Tomcat in fleet air defense. F/A-18 Hornets are currently operating in 37 tactical squadrons from air stations world-wide, and from 10 aircraft carriers. It is proudly flown by the U.S. Navy Blue Angels Flight Demonstration Squadron.

Features: The F/A-18 Hornet, an all-weather aircraft, is used as an attack aircraft as well as a fighter. In its fighter mode, the F/A-18 is used primarily as a fighter escort and for fleet air defense; in its attack mode, it is used for force projection, interdiction and close and deep air support.

Background: The F/A-18 Hornet demonstrated its capabilities and versatility during Operation Desert Storm, shooting down enemy fighters and subsequently bombing enemy targets with the same aircraft on the same mission, and breaking all records for tactical aircraft in availability, reliability, and maintainability. The aircraft's survivability was proven by Hornets taking direct hits from surface-to-air missiles, recovering successfully, being repaired quickly, and flying again the next day. The F/A-18 is a twin engine, mid-wing, multi-mission tactical aircraft. The F/A-18A and C are single seat aircraft. The F/A-18B and D are dual-seaters. The B model is used primarily for training, while the D model is the current Navy aircraft for attack, tactical control, forward air control and reconnaissance squadrons. The newest models, the E and F were rolled out at McDonnell Douglas on September 17, 1995, and are currently undergoing further testing at the Patuxent Naval Air Station in Maryland. The E is a single-seat while the F is a two-seater.

All F/A-18s can be configured quickly to perform either fighter or attack roles or both, through selected use of external equipment to accomplish specific missions. This "force multiplier" capability gives the operational commander more flexibility in employing tactical aircraft in a rapidly changing battle scenario. The fighter missions are primarily fighter escort and fleet air defense; while the attack missions are force projection, interdiction, and close and deep air support.

The F/A-18C and D models are the result of a block upgrade in 1987 incorporating provisions for employing updated missiles and jamming devices against enemy ordnance. C and D models delivered since 1989 also include an improved night attack capability.

GENERAL CHARACTERISTICS, C AND D MODELS

Primary Function: Multi-role attack and fighter aircraft

Contractor: Prime: McDonnell Douglas; Major Subcontractor: Northrop

Unit Cost: $24 million

Propulsion: Two F404-GE-402 enhanced performance turbofan engines

Thrust: 17,700 pounds (8,027 kg) static thrust per engine

Length: 56 feet (16.8 meters)

Height: 15 feet 4 inches (4.6 meters)

Maximum Takeoff Gross Weight: 51,900 pounds (23,537 kg)

Wingspan: 40 feet 5 inches (13.5 meters)

Range: (with external tanks): Fighter: 1,379 nautical miles (1,585.9 miles/2,537 km); Attack: 1,333 nautical miles (1,532.9 miles/2,453 km)

Ceiling: 50,000+ feet

Speed: Mach 1.7+

Crew: A, C and E models: one; B, D and F: two

Armament: One 20mm MK-61A1 Vulcan cannon; External Payload: AIM-9 Sidewinder, AIM-7 Sparrow, AIM-120 AMRAAM, Harpoon, Harm, Shrike, SLAM, SLAM-ER, Walleye, Maverick missiles; Joint Stand-Off Weapon (JSOW); Joint Direct Attack Munition (JDAM); various general purpose bombs, mines and rockets.

Date Deployed: First flight: November 1978; Operational, October 1983 (A/B models); September 1987 (C/D models)

GENERAL CHARACTERISTICS. E AMD F MODELS (SUPER HORNET)

Primary Function: Multi-role attack and fighter aircraft

Contractor: McDonnell Douglas

Unit Cost: $35 million

Propulsion: Two F414-GE-400 turbofan engines

Thrust: 22,000 pounds (9,977 kg) static thrust per engine

Length: 60.3 feet (18.5 meters)

Height: 16 feet (4.87 meters)

Maximum Takeoff Gross Weight: 66,000 pounds (29,932 kg)

Wingspan: 44.9 feet (13.68 meters)

Ceiling: 50,000+ feet

Speed: Mach 1.8+

Crew: A, C and E models: one; B, D and F models: two

Armament: One 20mm MK-61A1 Vulcan cannon; External payload: AIM-9 Sidewinder, AIM-7 Sparrow, AIM-120 AMRAAM, Harpoon, Harm, Shrike, SLAM, SLAM-ER, Walleye, Maverick missiles; Joint Stand-Off Weapon (JSOW); Joint Direct Attack Munition (JDAM); various general purpose bombs, mines and rockets.

First Flight: December 1995

P-3C ORION

Description: Lockheed four-engine propeller aircraft used as a submarine hunter and for surface surveillance.

Features: The P-3C Orion is a land-based, long range anti-submarine warfare (ASW) patrol aircraft. It has advanced submarine detection sensors such as directional frequency and ranging (DIFAR) sonobuoys and magnetic anomaly detection (MAD) equipment. The avionics system is integrated by a general purpose digital computer that support all of the tactical displays, monitors and automatically launches ordnance and provides flight information to the pilots. In addition, the system coordinates navigation information and accepts sensor data inputs for tactical display and storage. The P-3C can carry a mixed payload of weapons internally and on wing pylons.

Background: In February 1959, the Navy awarded Lockheed a contract to develop a replacement for the aging P-2 Neptune. The P3V Orion entered the inventory in July 1962, and over 30 years later it remains the Navy's sole land-based antisubmarine warfare aircraft. It has gone through one designation change (P-3V to P-3) and three major models: P-3A, P-3B, and P-3C, the latter being the only one now in active service. The last P-3 came off the production line at the Lockheed plant in April 1990.

GENERAL CHARACTERISTICS

Unit Cost: $36 million (FY 1987)

Propulsion: Four Allison T-56-A-14 turboprop engines (4,600 shaft horsepower each)

Length: 116 feet 8 inches (35.56 meters)

Wingspan: 99 feet 7 inches (29.9 meters)

Height: 33 feet 8 inches (10.26 meters)

Weight: Max gross take-off: 139,760 pounds (62,892 kg)

Speed: Maximum: 405 knots (466 mph, 745 kmph); Cruise: 350 knots (403 mph, 644kmph)

Ceiling: 30,000 feet (9,000 meters)

Range: Typical mission: 10-12 hours duration; Maximum endurance: 14 hours

Crew: 12

Armament: Harpoon (AGM-84) cruise missile; Maverick (AGM-65) air-to-ground missiles, MK-46 torpedoes, depth charges, sonobuoys; and mines up to around 20,000

pounds (9 metric tons) internal and external loads

Date Deployed: First flight, November 1959; Operational, P-3A August 1962; and P-3C August 1969

S-3 VIKING

Description: Jet aircraft, used to hunt and destroy enemy submarines and provide surveillance of surface shipping. The ES-3 version is fitted for electronic warfare and reconnaissance.

Features: The S-3A Viking replaced the S-2 Tracker and entered fleet service in 1974. The S-3 is a carrier-based, subsonic, all-weather, long-range, multi-mission aircraft. It operates primarily with carrier battle groups in anti-submarine warfare zones. It carries automated weapon systems and is capable of extended missions with in-flight refueling.

Background: The last production S-3A was delivered in August 1978. The inventory includes S-3As and S-3Bs. Also, sixteen S-3As were converted to ES-3As for carrier-based electronic surveillance.

GENERAL CHARACTERISTICS:

Primary Function: Antisubmarine warfare and sea surveillance

Contractor: Lockheed-California Company

Unit Cost: $27 million

Propulsion: Two General electric TF-34-GE-400B turbofan engines (9,275 pounds thrust each)

Length: 53 feet 4 inches (16 meters)

Wingspan: 68 feet 8 inches (20.6 meters)

Height: 22 feet 9 inches (6.9 meters)

Weight: Maximum design gross take-off: 52,539 pounds (23,643 kg)

Speed: 450 knots (518 mph, 828.8 kph)

Ceiling: 40,000 feet

Range: 2,300+ nautical miles (2,645 statute miles, 4,232 km)

Crew: Four

Armament: Up to 3,958 pounds (1,781 kg) of AG<-84 Harpoon missiles, rockets, torpedoes, mines and depth charges

Date Deployed: First flight, January 21, 1972; Operational, February 1974

CH-46D/E SEA KNIGHT

Service: Navy and Marine Corps

Description: Medium lift assault helicopter, primarily used to move cargo and troops.

Mission: The CH-46D Sea Knight helicopter is used by the Navy for shipboard delivery of cargo and personnel. The Ch-46E is used by the Marine Corps to provide all-weather, day or night assault transport of combat troops, supplies and equipment. Troop assault is the primary function and the movement of supplies and equipment is secondary. Additional tasks may be assigned, such as combat support, search and rescue, support of forward refueling and rearming points, aeromedic evacuation of casualties from the field and recovery of aircraft and personnel.

Background: The Ch-46 Sea Knight was first procured in 1964 to meet the medium-lift requirements of the Marine Corps in all combat and peacetime environments since that time. The Sea Knight fleet is currently being maintained until a suitable replacement is approved.

GENERAL CHARACTERISTICS

Primary Function: Medium lift assault helicopter

Contractor: Boeing Vertol Company

Power Plant: Two GE-T58-16 engines

Thrust: 1,770 hp

Length: 45 feet 7 inches (13.89 meters) with rotors folded

Width: 51 feet (15.54 meters) with rotors folded

Height: 16 feet 8 inches (5.08 meters)

Maximum Takeoff Weight: 34,300 pounds (11,032 kg)

Range: 132 nautical miles (151.8 miles) for land assault mission

Speed: 145 knots (166.75 miles per hour)

Ceiling: 10,000 + feet

Crew: Four: pilot, co-pilot, crew chief, mechanic

Payload: Combat: maximum of 22 troops and two aerial gunners; Medical Evacuation: 15 litters, two attendants; Cargo: 5,000 pounds (2,270 kg) maximum

Introduction Date: January 1978

CH-53A/D AND RH-53D SEA STALLION

Service: Navy and Marine Corps

Description: The CH-53A/D transports personnel, supplies and equipment in support of amphibious and shore operations. The RH-53D is used primarily for Airborne Mine Countermeasures (AMCM), with a secondary mission of shipboard delivery.

Background: The CH-53A was ordered in the early 1960s to satisfy a Marine Corps requirement for a heavy lift helicopter. Other variants of the H-53 and the RH-53P and the MH-53E, which are used for mine countermeasures. The H-53s can operate from carriers and other warships.

GENERAL CHARACTERISTICS A-D MODELS

Contractor: Sikorsky Aircraft Division of United Technologies Corp.

Propulsion: Two General Electric T64-GE-413 turboshaft engines (3,925 shaft horsepower each)

Length: Fuselage:67.5 feet (20.3 meters); Rotors turning: 88 feet 3 inches (26.5 meters)

Height: 24 feet 11 inches (7.2 meters)

Weight: 21 tons (max gross) (18.9 metric tons)

Main Rotor Diameter: 72 feet 3 inches (21.7 meters)

Range: 578 nautical miles (665 statute miles, 1,064 km); 886 nautical miles ferry range

Ceiling: 12,450 feet

Speed: 160 knots (184 mph, 294 kmph)

Load: 37 troops or 24 litter patients plus four attendants or 8,000 pounds (3,600 kg) cargo

Crew: Two pilots, one aircrewman (7 crewmen in RH-53D)

Armament: None

Date Deployed: First flight: October 14, 1964; Operational: November 1966

SH-2G SEASPRITE

Description: Ship-based helicopter with anti-submarine, anti-surface threat capability, including over-the-horizon targeting. This aircraft extends and increases shipboard sensor and weapon capabilities against several types of enemy threats, including submarines of all types, surface ships, and patrol craft that may be armed with anti-ship misiles.

Features: Seasprite's primary missions include anti-submarine and anti-surface warfare, anti-ship missile defense, and anti-ship surveillance and targeting. Secondary missions may include medical evacuation, search and rescue, personnel and cargo transfer, as well as small boat interdiction, amphibious assault air support, gun fire spotting, mine detection and battle damage assessment.

GENERAL CHARACTERISTICS

Primary Function: ASW, ASuW, ASMD, ASST

Contractor: Kaman

Unit Cost: $26 million

Propulsion: Two T700-GE-401/401C turboshaft engines

Length: 52 feet 9 inches (15.9 meters)

Fuselage Length: 40 feet 6 inches (12.2 meters)

Height: 15 feet (4.5 meters)

Weight: 9,110 pounds (4,099.5 kg) empty

Maximum Takeoff Weight: 13,500 pounds (6,075 kg) normal takeoff

Range: over 340 nautical miles (391 statute miles, 625.6 km) with maximum fuel

Ceiling: 10,000 feet at 13,500 pounds (6,075 kg)

Speed: 150 knots maximum (172.5 mph, 277.55 kmph)

Crew: Three

Armament: Two MK 46 or MK 50 torpedoes

Date Deployed: First flight: July 2, 1959 (SH-2); Operational: December 1964 (SH-2G)

SH-60 SEAHAWK

(Other versions are the UH-60 Black Hawk {Army}; HH-60H {Navy}; MH-60G Pave Hawk {Air Force}; HH-60J Jayhawk {Coast Guard}.

Service: Navy, Army, Air Forced, Coast Guard

Description: A twin-engine, medium lift, utility or assault helicopter.

Features: The Seahawk is a twin-engine helicopter. It is used for anti-submarine warfare, search and rescue, drug interdiction, anti-ship warfare, cargo lift, and special operations. The Navy's Sh-60B Seahawk is an airborne platform based aboard cruisers, destroyers, and frigates, and deploys sonobuoys (sonic detectors) and torpedoes in an anti-submarine role. They also extend the range of the ship's radar capabilities. The Navy's SH-60F is carrier-based. Some versions, such as the Air Force's MH-60G Pave hawk and the Coast Guard's HH-60J Jayhawk, are equipped with a rescue hoist with a 250 foot (75 meter) cable that has a 600 pound (270kg) lift capability, and a retractable in-flight refueling probe. The Army's UH-60L Black Hawk can carry 11 soldiers or 2,600 pounds (1,170 kg) of cargo or sling load 9,000 pounds (4,050 kg) of cargo.

Background: The UH-60 Black hawk was fielded by the Army in 1979. The Navy received the SH-60B Seahawk in 1983 and the SH-60F in 1988. The Air Force received the MH-60G Pave Hawk in 1982, while the Coast Guard received the HH-60J jayhawk in 1992. The unit cost varies with the version. For example, the unit cost of the Army's UH-60L Black Hawk is $5.9 million, while the unit cost of the Air Force MH-60G Pave Hawk is $10.2 million.

GENERAL CHARACTERISTICS:

Primary Function: Varies with the particular branch of military service

Contractor: Sikorsky Aircraft Corporation (airframe); General Electric Company (engines); IBM Corporation (avionics components)

Power Plant: Two General Electric T700-GE-700 or T700-GE-701C engines

Thrust: Up to 1,940 shaft horsepower

Length: 64 feet 10 inches (19.6 meters)

Height: Varies with the version; from 13 to 17 feet (3.9 to 5.1 meters)

Rotor Diameter: 53 feet 8 inches (16.4 meters)

Weight: Varies from 21,000 to 23,000 pounds (9,450 to 10,350 kg)

Speed: 180 knots maximum

Range: Generally about 380 nautical miles (600 km); unlimited with air refueling .

Armament: Usually two 7.62mm machine guns mounted in the windows; can also be equipped with three MK 46 or MK 50 torpedoes, or additional .50 caliber machine guns mounted in the doors.

Crew: Usually three or four

V-22A OSPREY

Service: Navy, Marine Corps and Air Force

Description: Multi-mission aircraft that combines vertical take-off and landing capability with high speed, high altitude flight.

Background: The Navy's HV-22A will provide combat search and rescue, delivery and retrieval of special warfare teams along with fleet logistic support transport. The Marine Corps' MV-22A will be an assault transport for troops, equipment, and supplies, operating from air capable ships or bases ashore.

Features: The Osprey is a tiltrotor aircraft with a 38-foot rotor system and engine/transmission nacelle mounted on each wing tip. It can operate as a helicopter when taking off and landing vertically. Once airborne, the nacelles rotate forward 90 degrees for horizontal flight, converting the V-22 to a high speed, fuel efficient turboprop airplane. The wing rotates for compact storage aboard ship. The first flight occurred in March 1989.

GENERAL CHARACTERISTICS

Primary Function: Vertical takeoff and landing (VTOL) aircraft

Contractor: Bell-Boeing

Propulsion: Two pivoting engines: T406-80-400

Main Rotor Diameter: 38 feet (11.58 meters)

Blades per Rotor: Three

Weight: Combat: 42,486 pounds (19,118.7kg); Landing: 33,615 pounds (15,126.75 kg)

Ceiling: 5,000 feet (1,524 meters) cruising altitude; 22,000 feet combat ceiling

Speed: 284 knots (326.6 mph; 522.56 kmph)

Armament: Provisions for two .50 caliber cabin guns

SURFACE CRAFT

AIRCRAFT CARRIERS — CV, CVN

Description: Aircraft carriers provide a wide range of possible response for the National Command Authority.

THE CARRIER MISSION

To provide a credible, sustainable, independent forward presence and conventional deterrence in peacetime,

To operate as the cornerstone of joint/allied maritime expeditionary forces in times of crisis, and

To operate and support aircraft attacks on enemies, protect friendly forces and engage in sustained independent operations of war.

Features: The aircraft carrier continues to be the centerpiece of the forces necessary for forward presence. Whenever there has been a crisis, the first question has been, "Where are the carriers?" Carriers support and operate aircraft that engage in attacks on airborne, afloat, and ashore targets that threaten free use of the sea, and engage in sustained operations in support of other forces.

Aircraft carriers are deployed worldwide in support of U.S. interests and commitments. They can respond to global crises in ways ranging from peacetime presence to full-scale war. Together with their on-board air wings, the carriers have vital roles across the full spectrum of conflict.

The Nimitz-class carriers, seven operational and two under construction, are the largest warships in the world. USS NIMITZ (CVN-68) will undergo its first refueling during a three-year Refueling Complex Overhaul at Newport News Shipbuilding in Newport News, Virginia, in 1998.

GENERAL CHARACTERISTICS, NIMITZ CLASS

Builder: Newport News Shipbuilding Co., Newport News, VA

Power Plant: Two nuclear reactors, four geared steam turbines, four shafts

Length: 1,040 feet (317 meters)

Flight Deck Width: 252 feet (76.8 meters)

Beam: 134 feet (40.84 meters)

Displacement: Approximately 97,000 tons (87.3 metric tons) full load

Speed: 30+ knots (34.5+ miles per hour)Aircraft: 85

Ships of the Class: 7 operational; 2 under construction

Crew: Ship's Company: 3,200; Air Wing: 2,480

Armament: Four NATO Sea Sparrow launchers, 20mm Phalanx CIWS mounts: (3 on Eisenhower and Nimitz; 4 on Vinson and later ships of the class)

Date Deployed: May 3, 1975 (USS NIMITZ)

GENERAL CHARACTERISTICS, ENTERPRISE CLASS

Builders: Newport News Shipbuilding Co., Newport News, VA

Power Plant: Eight nuclear reactors, four geared steam turbines, four shafts

Length: 1,040 feet (317 meters)

Flight Deck Width: 252 feet (75.6 meters)

Beam: 133 feet (39.9 meters)

Displacement: 89,600 tons (80,640 metric tons) full load

Speed: 30+ knots (34.5 miles per hour)

Aircraft: 85

SHIPS OF THE CLASS: 1

Crew: Ship's Company: 3,350; **Air Wing:** 2,480

Armament: Sea Sparrow Missile Launchers, Three Phalanx 20mm CIWS mounts

Date Deployed: November 25, 1961

GENERAL CHARACTERISTICS, JOHN F. KENNEDY CLASS

Builders: Newport News Shipbuilding, Newport News, VA

Power Plant: Eight boilers four geared steam turbines, four shafts, 280,000 total shaft horsepower

Length: 1,052 feet (315,6 meters)

Flight Deck Width: 252 feet (76.8 meters)

Beam: 130 feet (39.6 meters)

Displacement: 82,000 tons (full load)

Speed: 30+ knots (34.5 miles per hour)

Aircraft: Approximately 85

SHIPS OF THE CLASS: 1

Crew: Ship's Company: 3,117; Air Wing: 2,480

Armament: Sea Sparrow missiles with box launchers, three 20mm Phalanx CIWS mounts

Date Deployed: September 7, 1968

GENERAL CHARACTERISTICS, KITTY HAWK CLASS

Builders: CV-63, New York Ship Building Corporation, Camden, NJ; CV-64, New York Naval Shipyard, Brooklyn, NY

Power Plant: Eight boilers, four geared steam turbines, four shafts, 280,000 total shaft horsepower

Length: 1,062.5 feet (323.8 meters)

Flight Deck Width: 252 feet (76.8 meters)

Beam: 130 feet (39 meters)

Displacement: Approximately 80,800 tons (72,720 metric tons) full load

Speed: 30+ knots (34.5+ miles per hour)

Aircraft: 85

SHIPS OF THE CLASS: 2

Crew: Ship's Company:3,150; Air Wing: 2,480

Armament: Sea Sparrow launchers, 3 20mm Phalanx CIWS mounts

Date Deployed: April 29, 1961

GENERAL CHARACTERISTICS, FORRESTAL CLASS

Builders: New York Naval Shipyard, Brooklyn, NY

Power Plant: Eight boilers, four geared steam turbines, four shafts, 280,000 shaft horsepower

Length: 1,086 feet (317 meters)

Flight Deck Width: 252 feet (76.8 meters)

Beam: 129 feet (39.3 meters)

Displacement: Approximately 79,300 tons

Speed: 30+ knots (34.5+ miles per hour)

Aircraft: Approximately 75

SHIPS OF THE CLASS: 1

Crew: Ship's Company: 3,019; **Air Wing:** 2,480

Armament: Four NATO Sea Sparrow launchers; 3 20mm Phalanx CIWS mounts

Date Deployed: October 1, 1955

USS CONSTITUTION "OLD IRONSIDES"

Description: Wooden hull, three-masted frigate. The oldest commissioned ship in the U.S. Navy. One of six frigates authorized to form the United States Navy for use against the Barbary pirates.

Features: Built to be powerful enough to defeat an enemy of equivalent strength and fast enough to out-sail a stronger opponent.

GENERAL CHARACTERISTICS

Builders: Col. George Claghorn, Edmond Hartt's Shipyard, Boston, Massachusetts.

Unit Cost: $302,718 (1797 dollars)

Power Plant: 42,710 square feet of sail on three masts

Length: 204 feet (62.16 meters) (billet head to taffrail); 175 feet (53.32 meters) at waterline

Beam: 43.5 feet (13.25 meters)

Mast Height: Foremast, 198 feet (60.33 meters); mainmast, 220 feet (67.03 meters); mizzenmast, 172.5 feet (52.56 meters)

Displacement: 2,200 tons

Speed: 13+ knots (approximately 14.95 mph, 24kmph)

Crew: 450 including 55 Marines and 30 boys (1797)

Armament: 32 24-pounder long guns; 20 32-pounder carronades; and two 24-pounder bow chasers.

Boats: One 36-foot long boat; two 30-foot cutters; two 28-foot whaleboats; one 28-foot gig; one 22-foot jolly boat; and one 14-foot punt.

Anchors: Two main bowers (5,300 pounds); one sheet anchor (5,400 pounds); one stream anchor (1,100 pounds); and two kedge anchors (400 and 700 pounds).

Date Deployed: October 21, 1797

AMMUNITION SHIPS — AE

Description: Ammunition ships deliver munitions to warships.

Features: Ammunition ships keep the fleet supplied with ammunition and ordnance, indepen-

dently or with other combat logistics ships. Ammunition is delivered by slings on ship-to-ship cables, and by helicopters.

Background: The Navy's ammunition shops are all of the Kilauea class. The lead ship of the class, USNS KILAUEA (T-AE 26), and USNS BUTTE (T-AE 27, USNS FLINT (T-AE 32) and USNS KISKA (T-AE 35) are operated by the Military Sealift Command with civilian master and crew, but the remaining four are Navy manned with a commanding officer.

GENERAL CHARACTERISTICS, KILAUEA CLASS

Builders:

AE-27, General Dynamics, Quincy Shipbuilding Division;

AE-28, 29, Bethlehem Steel, Sparrows Point, Maryland;

AE-33 through AE-35, Ingalls Shipbuilding, Pascagoula,, Mississippi

Power Plant: Three boilers, geared turbines, one shaft, 22,000 shaft horsepower

Length: 564 feet (169.2 meters)

Beam: 81 feet (24.3 meters)

Displacement: Approximately 18,088 tons full load

Speed: 20 knots (23 mph, 36.8 kmph)

Aircraft: Two CH-46 Sea Knight helicopters

SHIPS OF THE CLASS: 6

Crew: 17 Officers, 366 Enlisted

Armament: Two Phalanx close-in weapons systems

Date Deployed: 14 December 1968 (USS Butte)

AMPHIBIOUS ASSAULT SHIPS — LHA, LHD, LPH

Description: Primary landing ships, resembling small aircraft carriers, designed to put troops on hostile shores.

Features: Modern U.S. Navy amphibious assault ships are called upon to perform as primary landing ships for assault operations of Marine expeditionary units. These ships use Landing Craft Air Cushion (LCAC), conventional landing craft and helicopters to move Marine assault forces ashore. In a secondary role, using AV-8B Harrier aircraft and antisubmarine warfare helicopters, these ships perform sea control and limited power projection missions.

Background: Amphibious warships are uniquely designed to support assault from the sea against defended positions ashore. They must be able to sail in harm's way and provide a rapid built-up of combat power ashore in the face of opposition. The United States maintains the largest and most capable amphibious force in the world. USS WASP

(LHD-1) is the largest amphibious ship in the world. This, the lead ship of its class, was commissioned in July 1989 in Norfolk, Virginia. Construction of the last ships of the class continues at Ingalls Shipbuilding, Pascagoula, Mississippi..

GENERAL CHARACTERISTICS, WASP CLASS

Builders: Ingalls Shipbuilding, Pascagoula, MS

Power Plant: Two boilers, two geared steam turbines, two shafts, 70,000 shaft horsepower

Length: 844 feet (253.2 meters)

Beam: 106 feet (31.9 meters)

Displacement: Approximately 40,500 tons (36,450 metric tons) full load

Speed: 20+ knots (23.5+ miles per hour)

Aircraft: Assault: 42 CH-46 Sea Knight Helicopters; Sea Control: 20 AV-8B Harrier attack planes; six ASW helicopters

SHIPS OF THE CLASS: 6

Crew: Ship's Company: 104 Officers, 1,004 Enlisted

Marine Detachment: 1,894

Armament: Two NATO Sea Sparrow launchers; three 20mm Phalanx CIWS mounts; eight .50 caliber machine guns

Date Deployed: July 29, 1989 (USS Wasp)

GENERAL CHARACTERISTICS, TARAWA CLASS

Builders: Ingalls Shipbuilding, Pascagoula, MS

Power Plant: Two boilers, two geared steam turbines, two shafts, 70,000 total shaft horsepower

Length: 820 feet (249.9 meters)

Beam: 106 feet (31.8 meters)

Displacement: 39,400 tons (35,460 metric tons) full load

Speed: 24 knots (27.6 mph)

Aircraft: (Actual mix depends upon mission). Nine CH-53 Sea Stallion helicopters; Twelve Ch-46 Sea Knight helicopters; Six AV-8B Harrier attack planes

SHIPS OF THE CLASS: 5

Crew: Ships Company: 82 Officers, 882 Enlisted

Marine Detachment: 1,900 plus

Armament: Two RAM launchers; two 5-inch/54 caliber MK-45 lightweight guns; two Phalanx 20 mm CIWS mount; six 25 mm MK 38 machine guns

Date Deployed: May 29, 1976 (USS Tarawa)

GENERAL CHARACTERISTICS, IWO JIMA CLASS

Builders: Philadelphia Naval Shipyard

Power Plant: Two boilers, one geared steam turbine, one shaft, 22,000 total shaft horsepower

Length: 598 feet (182.27 meters)

Flight Deck Width: 104 feet (31.2 meters)

Beam: 84 feet (25.2 meters)

Displacement: 17,000 tons (light load)

Speed: 23 knots (26.5 mph)

Aircraft: (Actual mix depends upon mission). 11 CH-53 Sea Stallions; 20 CH-46 Sea Knight helicopters

SHIPS OF THE CLASS: 3

Crew: Ships Company: 80 Officers, 638 Enlisted

Marine Detachment: 1,750

Armament: Two 20 mm Phalanx CIWS

Date deployed: August 26, 1961 (USS Iwo Jima)

AMPHIBIOUS COMMAND SHIPS — LCC

Description: Amphibious Command ships provide command and control for fleet commanders.

Background: Commissioned in 1970, these are the only ships to be designed initially for an amphibious command ship role. Earlier amphibious command ships lacked sufficient speed to keep up with a 20-knot amphibious force. Subsequently, both ships became fleet flagships. USS Blue Ridge became the Seventh Fleet command ship in 1979, and USS Mount Whitney became the Second Fleet command ship in 1981.

GENERAL CHARACTERISTICS, BLUE RIDGE CLASS

Builders: Philadelphia Naval Shipyard - LCC 19; Newport News Shipbuilding, Co. - LCC 20

Power Plant: Two boilers, one geared turbine, one shaft, 22,000 horsepower

Length Overall: 634 feet (190 meters)

Beam Extreme: 108 feet (32 meters)

Displacement: 18,874 tons (16,987 metric tons) full load

Speed: 23 knots (26.5 mph, 42.4 kmph)

Aircraft: All helicopters except the CH-53 Sea Stallion can be carried

SHIPS OF THE CLASS: 2

Crew: 52 Officers, 790 Enlisted

Date Deployed: 14 November 1970 (USS Blue Ridge)

AMPHIBIOUS TRANSPORT DOCK — LPD

Description: Troop transports for amphibious operations.

Features: The amphibious transports are used to transport and land Marines, their equipment and supplies by embarked landing craft or amphibious vehicles augmented by helicopters in amphibious assault.

Background: These versatile ships perform the mission of amphibious transports, amphibious cargo ships and the older LSDs. The Navy's newest class of ship, the LPD-17, is scheduled to replace the majority of the Navy's amphibious fleet. These modern amphibious command and control platforms integrate the latest in shipbuilding and warfighting technologies. A fleet of twelve San Antonio class ships is currently planned. The Navy announced the contract award for LPD-17 on December 17, 1996.

The LPD-17 will be a highly reliable, warfare capable ship and the most survivable amphibious ship ever put to sea. The design incorporates state-of-the-art self-defense capabilities, C4I, and reduced signature technologies. Reduced operational costs and adaptability to technological advances over its 40 year service life are key design objectives. LPD-17 also incorporates the latest quality of life standards for the embarked Marines and Sailors with the flexibility to accommodate women Marines and Sailors as part of the crew and embarked troops.

GENERAL CHARACTERISTICS, SAN ANTONIO CLASS

Builders: Avondale Industries, Inc., Bath Iron Works, General Dynamics, Hughes Aircraft Company, and Intergraph Corp.

Unit Cost: About $641 million

Power Plant: Four turbocharged marine diesels, two shafts

Length: 684 feet (208.5 meters)

Beam: 105 feet (31.9 meters)

Displacement: Approximately 24,900 tons (25,300 metric tons) full load

Speed: in excess of 22 knots (24.2 mph, 38.7kmph)

Aircraft: Up to four CH-46 Sea Knight helicopters; up to two CH-53 Sea Stallion helicopters; and up to two MV-22 Osprey tilt rotor aircraft

SHIPS OF THE CLASS: 3 (Contract Option)

Crew: Ships company: 32 Officers, 463 Enlisted; Marine Detachment: 720

GENERAL CHARACTERISTICS, AUSTIN CLASS

Builders:

LPD 4-6, New York naval Shipyard

LPD 7-8, Ingalls Shipbuilding

LPD 9, 10, 12-15, Lockheed Shipbuilding

Unit Cost: $235-$419 million

Power Plant: Two boilers, two steam turbines, two shafts, 24,000 shaft horsepower

Length: 570 feet (171 meters)

Beam: 84 feet (25.2 meters)

Displacement: Approximately 17,000 tons (15,300 metric tons) full load

Speed: 21 knots (24.2 mph, 38.7kmph)

Aircraft: Up to six CH-46 Sea Knight helicopters

SHIPS OF THE CLASS: 11

Crew: Ships Company: 24 Officers, 396 Enlisted; Marine Detachment: 900

Armament: Two MK 38 25mm guns; two Phalanx CIWS; and eight .50 caliber machine guns.

Date deployed: February 6, 1965 (USS Austin)

CRUISERS — CG, CGN

Description: Large combat vessel with multiple target response capability.

Features: Modern U.S. Navy guided missile cruisers perform primarily in a Battle Force role. These ships are multi-mission (AAW, ASW, ASUW) surface combatants capable of supporting carrier or battleship battle groups, amphibious forces, or of operating independently and as flagships of surface action groups. Due to their extensive combat capability, these ships have been designated as Battle Force Capable (BFC) units. The cruisers are equipped with Tomahawk ASM/LAM giving them additional long range strike mission capability.

Background: Technological advances in the Standard Missile coupled with the AEGIS combat system and vertical launch system (VLS) in Ticonderoga class cruisers, and the upgrading of older cruisers have increased the AAW capability of surface combatants to pinpoint accuracy from wave-top to zenith. The addition of Tomahawk ASM/LAM in the CG-47, CGN-36, and CGN-38 classes, has vastly complicated unit target planning for any potential enemy, and returned an offensive strike role to the surface forces that seemed to have been lost to air power at Pearl Harbor.

GENERAL CHARACTERISTICS, TICONDEROGA CLASS

Builders:

Ingalls Shipbuilding: CG 47-50, CG 52-57, 59, 62, 65-66, 68-69, 71-73

Bath Iron Works: CG 51, 58, 60-61, 63-64, 67, 70

Power Plant: General Electric LM 2500 gas turbine engines, 2 shafts, 80,000 shaft horsepower total

Length: 567 feet

Beam: 55 feet

Displacement: 9,600 tons (full load)

Speed: 30+ knots

Aircraft: Two SH-2 Seasprite (LAMPS) in CG 47-48; Two SH-60 Sea Hawk (LAMPS III

SHIPS OF THE TICONDEROGA CLASS: 27

Crew: 24 Officers, 340 Enlisted

Armament: Standard Missile (MR); Anti-submarine Rocket (ASROC); Tomahawk ASM/LAM; six MK-46 torpedoes (from two triple mounts); two 5-inch/54 caliber MK 445 lightweight guns; two Phalanx Close-In Weapons Systems (CIWS)

Date Deployed: 22 January 1983 (USS Ticonderoga)

GENERAL CHARACTERISTICS, VIRGINIA CLASS

Builders: Newport News Shipbuilding, Co.

Power Plant: Two General electric nuclear reactors, two geared turbines, two shafts

Length: 585 feet

Beam: 63 feet

Displacement: 11,000 tons (full load)

Speed: 30+ knots

Aircraft: None

Helicopter Landing Capability: None

SHIPS OF THE VIRGINIA CLASS: 2

Crew: 39 Officers, 539 Enlisted

Armament: Standard Missile (MR); eight Harpoon (from 2 quad launchers); eight Tomahawk ASM/LAM (from two armored box launchers); ASROC; six MK-46 torpedoes (from two triple mounts); two 5-inch/54 caliber MK 45 lightweight guns; two Phalanx close-in weapons systems

Date Deployed: September 11, 1976 (USS Virginia)

GENERAL CHARACTERISTICS, CALIFORNIA CLASS

Builders: Newport News Shipbuilding, Co.

Power Plant: Two General Electric nuclear reactors, two geared turbines, two shafts

Length: 596 feet

Beam: 61 feet

Displacement: 10,450 tons (full load)

Speed: 30+ knots

Aircraft: None

Helicopter Landing Capability: Landing area only, no support facilities

SHIPS OF THE CLASS: 2

Crew: 40 Officers, 544 Enlisted

Armament: Standard Missile (MR); eight harpoon (from 2 quad launchers); ASROC (from MK-16 box launcher); four MK-46 torpedoes (from single fixed tubes); two 5-inch/54 caliber MK 45 lightweight guns; two Phalanx close-in weapons system (CIWS)

Date Deployed: February 16, 1974 (USS California)

DESTROYERS — DD, DDG

Description: These fast warships help safeguard larger ships in a fleet or battle group.

Features: Destroyers and guided missile destroyers operate in support of carrier battle groups, surface action groups, amphibious groups and replenishment groups. Destroyers primarily perform anti-submarine warfare duty while guided missile destroyers are multi-mission (ASW, AAW, ASUW) surface combatants. The addition of the MK-41 vertical Launch System (VLS) or Tomahawk Armored Box Launchers (ABLs) to many Spruance class destroyers has greatly expanded the role of destroyers in strike warfare.

Background: Technological advances have improved the capability of modern destroyers culminating in the Arleigh Burke (DDG 51) class. Named for the Navy's most famous destroyer squadron combat commander and three-time Chief of Naval Operations, the Arleigh Burke was commissioned in July 1991 and was the most powerful surface combatant ever to put to sea. Like the larger Ticonderoga class cruisers, DDG 51's combat systems center around the AEGIS combat system and the SPY-ID, multi-function phased array radar. The combination of AEGIS, the Vertical Launching System, and advanced anti-submarine warfare system, advanced anti-aircraft missiles and Tomahawk ASM/LAM, the Burke class continues the revolution at sea.

Designed for survivability, DDG 51 incorporates al-steel construction and many damage control features resulting from lessons learned during the Falkland Islands War and from the accidental attack on USS Stark. Like most modern U.S. surface combatants, DDG 51 utilizes gas turbine propulsion. These ships replaced the older Charles F. Adams and Farragut-class guided missile destroyers.

The four Kidd-class guided missile destroyers are similar to the Spruance class, but have greater displacement and improved combat systems. These ships were built originally for use by Iran (when the Shah was in power) and the contract was canceled by the succeeding Iranian government. The U. S. navy acquired them in 1981 and 1982. Like the older guided missile cruisers, these ships have been upgraded to improve their anti-air warfare performance against the technologically advanced threat expected into the 21st century.

The Spruance class destroyers, the first large U.S. Navy warships to employ gas turbine engines as their main propulsion system, are undergoing extensive modernizing. The upgrade program includes addition of vertical launchers for advanced missiles on 24 ships of this class, in addition to an advanced ASW system and upgrading of its helicopter capability. Like the Kidd class, Spruance class destroyers are expected to remain a major part of the Navy's surface combatant force into the 21st century.

GENERAL CHARACTERISTICS, ARLEIGH BURKE CLASS

Builders: Bath Iron Works, Ingalls Shipbuilding

Power Plant: Four General Electric LM 2500-30 gas turbines, two shafts, 100,000 total shaft horsepower

Length: 466 feet (142 meters)

Beam: 59 feet (18 meters)

Displacement: 8,300 tons (7,470 metric tons) full load

Speed: 31 knots (35,7 mph, 57.1kmph)

Aircraft: None. LAMPS III electronics installed on landing deck for coordinated DDG 51/helo ASW operations

SHIPS OF THE CLASS: 19

Crew: 23 Officers, 300 Enlisted

Armament: Standard missile; Harpoon; Tomahawk ASM/LAM; six MK-46 torpedoes (from two triple tube mounts); one 5-inch/54 caliber Mk-45 lightweight gun; two 20mm Phalanx close-in weapons system (CIWS)

GENERAL CHARACTERISTICS, KIDD AND SPRUANCE CLASSES

Builder: Ingalls Shipbuilding

Power Plant: Four General Electric LM 2500 gas turbines, two shafts, 80,000 shaft horsepower

Length: 563 feet (171.6 meters)

Beam: 55 feet (16.8 meters)

Displacement: Kidd - 9,900 tons (8,910 metric tons) full load; Spruance - 9,100 tons (8,190 metric tons) full load

Speed: 33 knots (38 mph, 60.8 kmph)

Aircraft: Kidd - one Sh-2F Seasprite LAMPS helicopter; Spruance - two SH-60 Seahawk LAMPS III helicopters

SHIPS OF THE KIDD CLASS: 4

SHIPS OF THE SPRUANCE CLASS: 31

Crew: Kidd Class: 31 Officers, 332 Enlisted; Spruance Class: 30 Officers, 352 Enlisted

Armament: 8 Harpoon (from 2 quad launchers); Tomahawk ASM/LAM, VLS or ABL in Spruance; ASROC; six MK-46 torpedoes (from 2 triple tube mounts); two 5-inch/54 caliber MK-45 lightweight guns; two 20mm Phalanx CIWS.

Kidd only: Standard missiles; Spruance only: NATO Sea Sparrow point defense AAW missiles

Date Deployed:

June 27, 1981 (USS Kidd)

September 20, 1975 (USS Spruance)

DOCK LANDING SHIP — LSD

Description: Dock Landing Ships support amphibious operations, including landings via Landing Craft Air Cushion (LCAC), conventional landing craft and helicopters, onto hostile shores.

Background: These ships transport and launch amphibious craft and vehicles with their crews and embarked personnel in amphibious assault operations.

LSD-41 was specifically designed to operate LCAC vessels. It has the largest capacity for these landing craft (four) of any U.S. Navy amphibious platform. It will also provide docking and repair services for LCACs and for conventional landing craft.

In 1987, the navy requested $324.2 million to fund one LSD-41 (Cargo variant). The ship differs from the original LSD-41 by reducing its number of LCACs to two in favor of additional cargo capacity.

GENERAL CHARACTERISTICS, HARPERS FERRY CLASS

Builders: Avondale Industries, Inc., New Orleans, LA

Power Plant: Four Colt Industries, 16 cylinder diesels, two shafts, 33,000 shaft horsepower

Length: 609 feet (185.6 meters)

Beam: 84 feet

Displacement: 16,708 tons (15,030 metric tons) full load

Speed: 20+ knots (23.5 mph)

Landing Craft: Two Landing Craft, Air Cushion

SHIPS OF THE CLASS: 4

Crew: Ships Company: 22 Officers, 397 Enlisted; Marine Detachment: 402 plus 102 surge

Armament: Two 25mm Machine Guns; two 20mm Phalanx CIWS; six .50 caliber machine guns

Date deployed: 7 January 1995 (USS Harpers Ferry)

GENERAL CHARACTERISTICS, WHIDBEY ISLAND CLASS

Builders:

Lockheed Shipbuilding, Seattle, WA: LSD 41/43

Arondale Shipyards, New Orleans, LA: LSD 44 through 48

Power Plant: Four Colt Industries, 16 cylinder diesels, two shafts, 33,000 shaft horsepower

Length: 609 feet (185.6 meters)

Beam: 84 feet

Displacement: 15,939 tons (14,345 metric tons) full load

Speed: 20+ knots (23.5 mph)

Landing Craft: Four Landing Craft Air Cushion

SHIPS OF THE WHIDBEY ISLAND CLASS: 8

Crew: Ships Company: 22 Officers, 391 Enlisted; Marine Detachment: 402 plus 102 surge

Armament: Two 25mm machine guns; two 20mm Phalanx CIS mounts; six .50 caliber machine guns

Date Deployed: February 9, 1985 (USS Whidbey Island)

GENERAL CHARACTERISTICS, ANCHORAGE CLASS

Builders: Ingalls Shipbuilding, Pascagoula, MS - LSD 46; General Dynamics, Quincy, MA - LSD 37-40

Power Plant: Two 600 psi boilers, two geared steam turbines, two shafts, 24,000 total shaft horsepower

Length: 553 feet (168.6 meters)

Beam: 85 feet (25.9 meters)

Displacement: 14,000 tons (full load)

Speed: 22 knots (25.3 mph, 40.5 kmph)

Aircraft: none

SHIPS OF THE CLASS: 5

Crew: Ships Company: 18 Officers, 340 Enlisted; Marine Detachment: 330

Armament: Four 3-inch/50 caliber twin barrel guns; two 25mm machine guns; and two 20mm Phalanx CIWS

Date Deployed: March 15, 1969

FAST COMBAT SUPPORT SHIPS — AOE

Description: High-speed vessel, designed as oiler, ammunition and supply ship.

Features: The fast combat support ship (AOE) is the Navy's largest combat logistics ship. The AOE has the speed and armament to keep up with the carrier battle groups. It rapidly replenishes Navy task forces and can carry more than 177,000 barrels of oil, 2,150 tons of ammunition, 500 tons of dry stores and 250 tons of refrigerated stores. It receives petroleum products, ammunition and stores from shuttle ships and redistributes these items simultaneously to carrier battle group ships. This reduces the vulnerability of services ships by reducing alongside time. Congress appropriated the funds for the lead ship of the AOE 6 (Supply class) in 1987.

GENERAL CHARACTERISTICS, SUPPLY CLASS

Builders: National Steel and Shipbuilding Co., San Diego, CA

Power Plant: Four General Electric LM 2500 gas turbines; 2 shafts; 105,000 shaft horsepower

Length: 754 feet (229.9 meters)

Beam: 107 feet (32.6 meters)

Displacement: 48,800 tons full load

Speed: 25 knots

Aircraft: Three CH-46 Sea Knight helicopters

SHIPS OF THE CLASS: 4

Crew: 40 Officers, 627 Enlisted

Armament: NATO Sea Sparrow missiles, two Phalanx CIWS, two 25mm machine guns

Date Deployed: February 26, 1994 (USS Supply)

GENERAL CHARACTERISTICS, SACRAMENTO CLASS

Builders:

AOE 1, 3, 4: Puget Sound naval Shipyard

AOE 2: New York Shipbuilding

Unit Cost: $458- $568 million

Power Plant: Four boilers, geared turbines, two shafts, 100,000 shaft horsepower

Length: 793 feet (237.9 meters)

Beam: 107 feet (32.1 meters)

Displacement: 53,000 tons full load

Speed: 26 knots (30 mph, 48 kmph)

Aircraft: Two CH-46 E Sea Knight helicopters

SHIPS OF THE CLASS: 4

Crew: 24 Officers, 576 Enlisted

Armament: NATO Sea Sparrow missiles, two Phalanx CIWS.

Date Deployed: March 14, 1964 (USS Sacramento)

FRIGATES

Description: Frigates fulfill a Protection of Shipping (POS) mission as Anti-Submarine Warfare (ASW) combatants for amphibious expeditionary forces, underway replenishment groups and merchant convoys.

Background: The guided missile frigates (FFG) bring an Anti-Air Warfare (AAW) capability to the frigate mission, but they have some limitations. Designed as cost-efficient surface combatants, they lack the multi-mission capability necessary for modern surface combatants faced with multiple, high-technology threats. They also offer limited capacity for growth. Despite this, the FFG-7 class is a robust platform, capable of withstanding considerable damage. This "toughness" was aptly demonstrated when USS Samuel B. Roberts struck a

mine and USS Stark was hit by two Exocet cruise missiles. In both cases the ships survived, were repaired and have returned to the fleet.

Two FFG-7 class ships have been decommissioned as of January 1996, and several more are planned to be decommissioned and transferred to foreign navies.

The Surface Combatant Force requirement Study does not define any need for a single mission ship such as the frigate, and there are no frigates planned in the navy's five-year shipbuilding plan.

GENERAL CHARACTERISTICS, OLIVER HAZARD PERRY CLASS

Builders:

Bath Iron Works: FFG 7-8, 11, 13, 15-16, 26, 29, 32, 34, 39, 42, 45, 47, 49, 50, 53, 55-56, 58-59,

Todd Shipyards, Seattle, WA: FFG 10, 20, 22, 28, 31, 37, 40, 48, 52.

Todd Shipyards, San Pedro, CA: FFG 9, 12, 14, 19, 23, 30, 33, 38, 41, 43, 46, 51, 54, 57, 60-61.

Power Plant: Two General Electric LM 2500 gas turbine engines, 1 shaft, 41,000 shaft horsepower

Length: 445 feet (133.5 meters); 453 feet (135.9 meters) with LAMPS III modification.

Beam: 45 feet (13.5 meters)

Displacement: 4,100 tons (full load)

Speed: 39+ knots (33.4+ mph)

Aircraft: Two SH-60 LAMPS III in FFG 8, 28, 29, 32, 33, 36-61; One Sh-2F (LAMPS MK-I) in FFG 7, 9-27, 30-31, 34.

SHIPS OF THE CLASS: 44

Crew: 13 Officers, 287 Enlisted

Armament: Standard Missile (MR); Harpoon (from Standard Missile Launcher); six MK-46 torpedoes (from two triple tube mounts); one 76mm (3-inch)/62 caliber MK 75 rapid fire gun; one Phalanx CIWS

Date Deployed: December 17, 1977 (USS Oliver Hazard Perry)

FLEET OILERS — AO

Description: Fleet oilers furnish ordnance, fuel and petroleum products to the fleet at sea during underway replenishments.

Features: Fleet oilers operate as a unit of an underway replenishment group, replenishing petroleum products and ordnance to the fleet at sea during underway replenishments (UNREPS). The oilers transport bulk petroleum and lubricants from depots to the ships of the battle group. The number of Navy-manned fleet oilers has decreased as more and more Military Sealift Command ships, manned by a civilian crew and commanded by a civilian master, have assumed responsibilities for supplying deployed ships.

GENERAL CHARACTERISTICS, CIMARRON CLASS

Builders: Avondale Shipyards

Power Plant: Two boilers, one steam turbine, one shaft, 24,000 shaft horsepower

Length: 708 feet (212.4 meters)

Beam: 88 feet (26.4 meters)

Displacement: 37,840 tons (34,083 metric tons) full load

Speed: 20 knots (23 mph, 36.8kmph)

Cargo Capacity: 180,000 barrels fuel; 600 tons of cargo ammunition

SHIPS OF THE CLASS: 5

Crew: 15 Officers, 318 Enlisted

Armament: Two Phalanx CIWS (except AO-178)

Date Deployed: January 10, 1981 (USS Cimarron)

HOSPITAL SHIPS — T-AH

Description: The hospital ships (T-AH) provide emergency, on-site combat surgical and medical care to U.S. deployed forces in wartime or a contingency.

Features: The two hospital ships are part of the Military Sealift Command's Strategic Sealift Force. Each ship contains 1,000 hospital beds, 12 operating rooms, radiological services, medical laboratories, an optometry lab, a pharmacy, and two oxygen producing plants. These ships are larger than any shore-based naval medical facility and each has a helo deck large enough to receive injured personnel from even the largest military helicopters.

Ordinarily, the ships are kept in reduced operating status and maintained by a small crew of civilian mariners and a Navy cadre crew of medical and communications specialists. They can be activated, fully manned, and ready to get underway in only five days. When activated, each has more than 800 active duty Navy personnel from the Navy's medical organization, 380 Navy support and communications personnel and 62 U.S. Civil Service mariners to operate the ship.

Background: The hospital ships are converted San Clemente-class tankers. USNS Mercy was delivered to the Navy in December 1986, and USNS Comfort was delivered in 1987. Both ships were activated for Operation Desert Storm to provide medical support for U.S. forces assigned to the Middle East.

GENERAL CHARACTERISTICS

Conversion: National Steel and Shipbuilding Co., San Diego, CA

Power Plant: Geared steam turbine, two boilers, one shaft, 24,500 shaft horsepower

Length: 894 feet

Beam: 106 feet

Displacement: 69,360 tons (full load)

Speed: 17.5 knots

SHIPS: 2

Crew: 62 civilian mariners, 387 Navy support and communications personnel, and 820 Navy medical personnel

Capacity: 1,000 beds; 12 operating rooms

Date deployed: December 1986 (USNS Mercy)

LANDING CRAFT, AIR CUSHIONED

Description: Air cushion craft for transporting ship-to-shore and across the beach, personnel, weapons, equipment, and cargo of the assault elements of the Marine Air-Ground Task Force.

Features: The landing craft air cushion (LCAC) is a high-speed, over-the-beach fully amphibious landing craft capable of carrying a 60-ton payload. It is used to transport weapons systems, equipment, cargo and personnel from ship to shore and across the beach. The advantages of air-cushion landing craft are numerous. They can carry heavy payloads, such as an M-1 tank, at high speeds. Their payload and speed mean more forces reach the shore in a shorter time, with shorter intervals between trips. The air cushion allows this vehicle to reach more than 70 percent of the world's coastline, while conventional landing craft can land at only 15 percent of the coasts.

Background: Thirty-three air-cushion landing craft were authorized and appropriated through FY86. An additional 15 were funded in FY89, 12 more in FY90 and FY91. The remaining 24 were funded in FY92. As of December 1995, 82 LCACs had been delivered to the Navy.

GENERAL CHARACTERISTICS

Class: LCAC-1

Builders: Textron Marine and Land Systems/ Avondale Gulfport Marine

Power Plant: Four Avco-Lycoming gas turbines rated at 3,955 shaft horsepower (max continuous); two shrouded reversible-pitch propellers; four 63-inch diameter double-entry fans.

Length: 87 feet 11 inches (26.4 meters)

Beam: 47 feet (14.1 meters)

Displacement: 151 tons (135.9 metric tons) full load

Range: 200 miles at 40 knots with payload

Speed: 40+ knots (46+ mph, 73.6kmph) with payload

Load Capacity: 60 tons/75 ton overload

Crew: Five

Armament: (Gun mounts will support) M-2HB .50 caliber machine gun; MK-19 Mod 3 40mm grenade launcher; M-60 machine gun.

Date Deployed: 1982

MARK V SPECIAL OPERATIONS CRAFT

Description: The MARK V is used to carry Special Operations Forces (SOF), primarily SEAL combat swimmers, into and out of operations where the threat to these forces is considered to be low to medium. They also support limited coastal patrol and interrption of enemy activities.

Background: The MARK V Special Operations Craft (SOC) is the newest, versatile, high performance combatant craft introduced into the Naval Special Warfare (NSW) Special Boat Squadron (SBR) inventory to improve maritime special operations capabilities.

MARK Vs are organized into detachments comprised of two boats, crews, and a deployment support package mounted on cargo transporters. The detachment can be delivered in-theater rapidly by two C-5 aircraft, by a well or flight deck equipped surface ship, and, if appropriate, under their own power. The detachment can be deployable within 48 hours of notification and ready for operations within 24 hours of arrival at a forward operating base. They can operate from shore facilities, from well-deck equipped ships or from ships with appropriate crane and deck space capabilities.

The MARK Vs are a result of a streamlined acquisition effort managed by the United Sates Special Operations Command (USSOCOM) Special Operations Acquisition Executive (SOAE). From the awarding of the contract to actual possession of the first boat took only 18 months.

GENERAL CHARACTERISTICS

Length: 82 feet

Beam: 17 feet 6 inches

Weight: 57 tons

Speed: 50 knots

MINEHUNTERS COASTAL — MHC

Description: Ships designed to clear mines from vital waterways.

Background: In the early 1980s, the U.S. Navy began development of a new mine countermeasures (MCM) force, which included two new classes of ships and minesweeping helicopters. The vital importance of a state-of-the-art mine countermeasures force was strongly underscored in the Persian Gulf during eight years of the Iran-Iraq war, and in Operation Desert Shield and Desert Storm in 1990 and 1991.

Osprey (MHC 51) class ships are mine hunter-killers capable of finding, classifying and destroying moored and bottom mines. The MHC 51 has a 15-day endurance and depends on a support ship or shore based facilities for resupply.

Avenger class ships are also designed as mine hunter-killers.

These ships use sonar and video systems, cable cutters and a mine detonating device that can be released and detonated by remote control. They are also capable of conventional sweeping measures. The ships' hulls are made of glass-reinforced plastic (GRP) fiberglass. They are the first large mine countermeasures ships built in the United States in nearly 27 years.

GENERAL CHARACTERISTICS, OSPREY CLASS

Builders:

MHC 51, 52, 55, 58-60: Intermarine USA, Savannah, GA

MHC 53-54, 56-57: Avondale Industries, Inc., Gulfport, MS

Power Plant: Two diesels (800 hp each); two Voith-Schneider (cycloidal) propulsion systems

Length: 188 feet (57.3 meters)

Beam: 36 feet (11 meters)

Displacement: 893 tons (804 metric tons) full load

Speed: 10 knots (18.4 kmph)

SHIPS OF THE CLASS: 12

Crew: 5 Officers, 46 Enlisted

Armament: Two .50 caliber machine guns; Mine Neutralization System, and other mine countermeasures systems

Date Deployed: 20 November 1993 (USS Osprey)

MINE COUNTERMEASURES SHIPS — MCM

Description: Ships designed to clear mines from vital waterways.

Background: In the early 1980s, the U.S. Navy began development of a new mine countermeasures (MCM) force, which included two new classes of ships and minesweeping helicopters. The vital importance of a state-of-the-art mine countermeasures force was strongly underscored in the Persian Gulf during the eight years of the Iran-Iraq war, and in Operation Desert Shield and Desert Storm in 1990 and 1991 when the Avenger (MCM 1) and Guardian (MCM 5) ships conducted MCM operations.

Avenger class ships are designed as mine hunter-killers capable of finding, classifying and destroying moored and bottom mines. The last three MCM ships were purchased in 1990, bringing the total to 14 fully deployable, oceangoing Avenger class ships. These ships use sonar and video systems, cable cutters and a mine detonating device that can be released and detonated by remote control. They are also capable of conventional sweeping measures. The ships are of fiberglass-sheathed, wooden hull construction. They are the first large mine countermeasures ships built in the United States in nearly 27 years. Osprey (MHC 51) class ships are also designed as mine hunter-killers. The MHC 51 has a 15-day endurance and depends on a support or shore-based facilities for resupply.

GENERAL CHARACTERISTICS, AVENGER CLASS

Builders: Peterson Shipbuilders, Sturgeon Bay, WI; Marinette Marine, Marinette, WI

Power Plant: Four diesels (600 horsepower each), two shafts with controllable pitch propellers

Length: 224 feet (68.28 meters)

Beam: 39 feet (11.89 meters)

Displacement: 1,312 tons (1,180.8 metric tons) full load

Speed: 14 knots (16.1 mph, 25.76 kmph)

SHIPS OF THE CLASS: 14

Crew: 8 Officers, 76 Enlisted

Armament: Mine neutralization system; Two .50 caliber machine guns

Date Deployed: September 12, 1987 (USS Avenger)

PATROL COASTAL BOATS — PC

Description: The primary mission of these ships is coastal patrol and interdiction surveillance, an important aspect of littoral operations outlined in the navy's strategy, "Forward . . . From the Sea." These ships also provide full mission support for Navy SEALs and other special operations forces.

Background: The Cyclone-class ships are assigned to Naval Special Warfare. Of the thirteen ships, nine operate out of the Naval Amphibious Base, Little Creek, Virginia, and four operate from the Naval Amphibious Base, Coronado, California. These ships provide the Naval Special Warfare Command with a fast, reliable platform that can respond to emergent requirements in a low intensity conflict environment.

GENERAL CHARACTERISTICS , CYCLONE CLASS

Builders: Bollinger Shpyards, Inc.

Power Plant: Four Paxman diesel engines; four shafts, 3,350 shaft horsepower

Length: 170 feet (51.82 meters)

Beam: 25 feet (7,62 meters)

Displacement: 331 tons (364.86 metric tons) full load

Speed: 35 knots (40 mph, 65kmph)

SHIPS OF THE CLASS: 13

Crew: Four Officers, 24 Enlisted, Eight Special Forces personnel

Armament: Two Mark 38 25mm machine guns; two .50 caliber machine guns; two Mark 19 automatic grenade launchers; six Stinger missiles.

RESCUE AND SALVAGE SHIPS — ARS

Description: Rescue and salvage ships render assistance to disabled ships, provide towing, salvage, diving, firefighting and heavy lift capabilities.

Features: The mission of the rescue and salvage ships is four-fold: to debeach stranded vessels, heavy lift capability from ocean depths, towing of other vessels, and manned diving operations. For rescue missions, these ships are equipped with fire monitors forward and amidships which can deliver either fire-fighting foam or sea water. The salvage holds of these ships are outfitted with portable equipment to provide assistance to other vessels in dewatering, patching, supply of electrical power and other essential service required to return a disabled ship to an operating condition.

Background: The U.S. Navy has responsibility for salvaging U. S. government-owned ships and, when it is in the best interests of the United States, privately-owned vessels as well. The rugged construction of these steel-hulled ships, combined with speed and endurance, make these rescue and salvage ships well-suited for rescue/salvage operations of Navy and commercial shipping throughout the world. The versatility of this class of ship adds immeasurably to the capabilities of the United States Navy with regard to rendering assistance to those in peril on the high seas.

GENERAL CHARACTERISTICS, SAFEGUARD CLASS

Primary Function: Firefighting, combat salvage, rescue towing, diving

Builders: Peterson Builders

Power Plant: Four Caterpiller 399 Diesels, two shafts, 4,200 horsepower

Length: 255 feet (77.7 meters)

Beam: 51 feet (15.5 meters)

Draft: 16 feet 9 inches (5.11 meters)

Displacement: 3,282 tons (3,230 metric tons) full load

Speed: 14 knots (16.1 mph, 25.8 kmph)

Endurance: 8,000 miles (12,672 km) at 8 knots (9,2kmph)

Salvage Capability: 7.5-ton capacity boom forward; 40-ton capacity boom aft

Heavy Lift: Capable of hauling force of 150 tons

Diving Depth: 190 feet (57.9 meters), using air

SHIPS OF THE CLASS: 4

Crew: 6 Officers, 94 Enlisted

Armament: Two .50 caliber machine guns; two MK-38 25mm guns

Date Deployed: August 16, 1985

SEA SHADOW

Description: Sea Shadow is a test craft developed under a combined program by the Advanced Research Projects Agency (ARPA), the Navy, and Lockheed Missiles and Space Company.

Background: The Sea Shadow program was begun in the mid-1980s. Its purpose is to explore a variety of new technologies for surface ships, including ship control, structures, automation for reduced manning, safekeeping and signature control.

GENERAL CHARACTERISTICS, SEA SHADOW

Power Plant: Diesel electric

Length: 164 feet (49.99 meters)

Beam: 68 feet (20.73 feet)

Draft: 14.5 feet (4.42 meters)

Displacement: 560 long tons (551.15 metric tons) full load

Crew: 10

TANK LANDING SHIPS — LST

Description: Tank Landing Ships (LST) are used to transport and land tanks, amphibious vehicles and other rolling stock in amphibious assault.

Features: Ships of this class are the first to depart from the bow-door design that characterized the workhorses of World War II. The hull form necessary to attain the 20-knot speeds of contemporary amphibious squadrons would not permit bow doors. Accordingly, these ships off-load cargo and vehicles by means of a 112-foot ramp over their bow. A stern gate allows off-loading of amphibious vehicles directly into the water. The two ships of the class, now assigned to the Naval Reserve Force, are the only of this 20-ship class of LSTs remaining in the fleet.

GENERAL CHARACTERISTICS, NEWPORT CLASS

Builders: National Steel and Shipbuilding

Power Plant: Six diesels, two shafts, 16,000 brake horsepower

Length: 522 feet (156.6 meters)

Beam: 69 feet (20.7 meters)

Displacement: 8,450 tons full load

Speed: 20 knots (23 mph, 36.8 kmph)

SHIPS OF THE CLASS: 2

Crew: 13 Officers, 244 Enlisted

Armament: One Phalanx 20 mm CIWS mount; two 25 mm MK 38 machine guns

Date Deployed: June 7, 1969 (USS Newport)

SUBMARINES

ATTACK SUBMARINES — SSN

Description: Attack submarine, designed to seek and destroy enemy submarines and surface ships.

Background: The concept of technical superiority over numerical superiority was and still is the driving force in American submarine development. A number of Third World countries are acquiring modern state-of-the-art non-nuclear submarines. Countering this threat in the primary mission of U.S. nuclear attack submarines. Their other missions range from intelligence collection and special forces delivery to anti-ship and strike warfare. The Navy began construction of Seawolf class submarines in 1989. Seawolf is designed to be exceptionally quiet, fast, well-armed with advanced sensors. It is a multi-mission vessel, capable of deploying to forward ocean areas to search out and destroy enemy submarines and surface ships and to fire missiles in support of other forces. The first of the class, Seawolf (SSN 21), completed its initial sea trials in July 1996. Attack submarines also carry the Tomahawk cruise missile. Tomahawk launches from attack submarines were successfully conducted during Operation desert Storm. The Benjamin Franklin class were converted from Fleet Ballistic Missile submarines and carry drydock shelters. They are equipped for special operations and support SEALs. The former missile spaces have been converted to accommodations, storage, and recreation spaces.

GENERAL CHARACTERISTICS, SEAWOLF CLASS

Builders: General Dynamics Electric Boat Division

Power Plant: One nuclear reactor, two geared steam turbines, one shaft

Length: 353 feet (107.6 meters)

Draft: 35 feet (10.67 meters)

Beam: 40 feet (12.2 meters)

Displacement: Approximately 9,150 tons (10,086 metric tons) submerged

Speed: 25+ knots (28+ miles per hour; 46.3+ kmph)

SHIPS OF THE CLASS: 3

Crew: 12 Officers; 121 Enlisted

Armament: Harpoon and Tomahawk missiles, VLS tubes, MK-48 torpedoes, four torpedo tubes.

GENERAL CHARACTERISTICS, LOS ANGELES CLASS

Builders: Newport News Shipbuilding Co.; General Dynamics Electric Boat Division.

Power Plant: One nuclear reactor, two geared steam turbines, one shaft

Length: 360 feet (109.73 meters)

Beam: 33 feet (10.06 meters)

Displacement: Approximately 6,900 tons (6,210 metric tons) submerged

SHIPS OF THE CLASS: 57

Speed: 20= knots (23+ mph, 36.8kmph)

Crew: 13 Officers; 116 Enlisted

Armament: Harpoon and Tomahawk missiles, VLS tubes, MK-48 torpedoes, four torpedo tubes.

Date Deployed: November 13, 1976 (USS Los Angeles)

GENERAL CHARACTERISTICS, NARWHAL CLASS

Builder: General Dynamics' Electric Boat Division

Power Plant: One nuclear reactor, two geared steam turbines, one shaft

Length: 314 feet (95.71 meters)

Beam: 38 feet (11.58 meters)

Displacement: Approximately 5,350 tons (4,815 metric tons) submerged

Speed: 20+ knots (23+mph, 36.8+ kmph)

Ships: USS NARWHAL (SSN-671), Norfolk VA

Crew: 13 Officers, 116 Enlisted

Armament: Harpoon and Tomahawk missiles, MK 48 torpedoes; four torpedo tubes.

Date Deployed: July 12, 1969 (USS Narwhal)

GENERAL CHARACTERISTICS, STURGEON CLASS

Builders: General Dynamics Electric Boat Division; General Dynamics, Quincy Shipbuilding Division; Ingalls Shipbuilding; Portsmouth Naval Shipyard; San Francisco Naval Shipyard; and Newport News Shipbuilding, Co.

Power Plant: One nuclear reactor, two steam turbines, one shaft

Length: 292 feet (89 meters), (SSN 667-677); 300 feet (91.44 meters, (SSN 678-687)

Beam: 32 feet (9.75 meters)

Displacement: Approximately 4,640 tons (4,176 metric tons) submerged

Speed: 20+ knots (23+ mph, 36.8 kmph)

SHIPS OF THE CLASS: 19

Crew: 12 Officers, 95 Enlisted

Armament: Harpoon, Tomahawk, MK-48 torpedoes, four torpedo tubes.

Date Deployed: March 3, 1967 (USS Sturgeon)

GENERAL CHARACTERISTICS, BENJAMIN FRANKLIN CLASS

Builders: Mare Island Naval Shipyard; General Dynamics Electric Boat Division

Power Plant: One nuclear reactor, two steam turbines, one shaft

Length: 425 feet (129.5 meters)

Beam: 33 feet (10.1 meters)

Displacement: Approximately 8,250 tons (7,425 metric tons) submerged

Speed: 20+ knots (23+ mph, 36.8+kmph)

SHIPS OF THE CLASS: 2

Armament: MK-48 torpedoes, four torpedo tubes

Date Deployed: October 22, 1965 (USS Benjamin Franklin)

FLEET BALLISTIC MISSILE SUBMARINES — SSBN

Description: Nuclear-powered submarine armed with long-range strategic missiles.

Background: strategic deterrence has been the sole mission of the fleet ballistic missile submarine (SSBN) since its inception in 1960, The SSBN provides the nation's most survivable and enduring nuclear strike capability. The Ohio class submarine replaced aging fleet ballistic missile submarines built in the 1960s and is far more capable.

Ohio class Trident ballistic missile submarines provide the sea-based "leg" of the triad of U.S. strategic offensive forces. By the turn of the century, the 18 Trident SSBNs (each carrying 24 missiles), will carry 50 percent of the total U.S. strategic warheads. Although the missiles have no pre-set targets when the submarine goes on patrol, the SSBNs are capable of rapidly targeting their missiles should the need arise, using secure and constant at-sea communications links.

Features: The first eight Ohio class submarines (Tridents) were originally equipped with 24 Trident I C-4 ballistic missiles. Beginning with the ninth Trident submarine, USS Tennessee (SSBN 734), all new ships are equipped with the Trident II D-5 missile system as they are built, and the earlier ships are being retrofitted to Trident II. Trident II can deliver significantly more payload than Trident I C-4 and more accurately.

The Ohio class submarines are specifically designed for extended deterrent patrols. To increase the time in port for crew turnover and replenishment, three large logistics hatches are fitted to provide large diameter resupply and repair openings. These hatches allow sailors to rapidly transfer supply pallets, equipment replacement modules and machinery components, significantly reducing the time required for replenishment and maintenance. The class design and modern main concepts allow the submarines to operate for 15+ years between overhauls.

GENERAL CHARACTERISTICS, OHIO CLASS

Builders: General Dynamics Electric Boat Division

Power Plant: One nuclear reactor, two geared steam turbines, one shaft

Length: 560 feet (179=0.69 meters)

Beam: 42 feet (10.06 meters)

Displacement: Approximately 18,700 tons (16,830 metric tons) submerged

Speed: 20+ knots (23+ mph, 36.8 kmph)

SHIPS OF THE CLASS: 16

Homeported at the Naval Submarine Base, Bangor, Washington:

Crew: 15 Officers, 140 Enlisted

Armament: 24 tubes for Trident I and II, MK-48 torpedoes, four torpedo tubes.

Date Deployed: November 11, 1981 (USS Ohio)

NR-1 DEEP SUBMERGENCE CRAFT

Description: A nuclear powered ocean engineering and research submarine.

Background: NR-1, the first deep submergence vessel using nuclear power, was launched at Groton, Connecticut on January 25, 1969, and successfully completed her initial sea trials August 19, 1969. It maneuvers by four ducted thrusters, two in the front and two in the rear. The vehicle also has planes mounted on the sail and a conventional rudder.

NR-1's missions have included search, object recovery, geological survey, oceanographic research, and installation and maintenance of underwater equipment. NR-1's unique capability to remain at one site and completely map or search an area with a high degree of accuracy has been a valuable asset on several occasions.

Following the loss of the Space Shuttle Challenger in 1986, the NR-1 was used to search for, identify, and recover critical parts of the Challenger raft. Because it can remain on the sea floor without resurfacing frequently, NR-1 was a major tool for searching deep waters. NR-1 remained submerged and on station even when heavy weather and rough seas hit the area and forced all other search and recovery ships into port.

Today, NR-1 continues to provide a valuable service to the Navy and many research and educational institutions.

Features: The NR-1 performs underwater search and recovery, oceanographic research missions and installation and maintenance of underwater equipment, to a depth of almost half a mile. Its features include extendable bottoming wheels, three viewing ports, exterior lighting and television and still cameras for color photographic studies, an object recovery claw, a manipulator that can be fitted with various gripping and cutting tools and a work basket that can be used in conjunction with the manipulator to deposit or recover items in the sea. Surface vision is provided through the use of a television periscope permanently installed on a mast in her sail area.

NR-1 has sophisticated electronics and computers that aid in navigation, communications, and object location and identification. It can maneuver or hold a steady position on or close to the seabed or underwater ridges, detect and identify objects at a considerable distance, and lift objects off the ocean floor.

NR-1 can travel submerged at approximately four knots for long periods, limited only by its supplies. It can study and map the ocean bottom, including temperature, currents, and other information for military, commercial and scientific uses. Its nuclear propulsion provides independence from surface support ships and essentially unlimited endurance. NR-1 is generally towed to and from remote mission locations by an accompanying surface tender, which is also capable of conducting research in conjunction with the submarine.

GENERAL CHARACTERISTICS

Primary Function: Deep submergence research and engineering vehicle

Hull Number: NR-1

Class: No class; this is a one-of-a-kind ship

Builder: General Dynamics Electric Boat Division

Power Plant: One nuclear reactor, one turbo-alternator; two motors (external), two propellers, four ducted thrusters (two horizontal, two vertical)

Length: 150 feet (45.72 meters)

Displacement: 400 tons (360 metric tons)

Beam: 12 feet (4.18 meters)

Maximum Operating Depth: 2,375 feet (724 meters)

Crew: 2 Officers, 3 Enlisted, 2 Scientists

Armament: None

Date Deployed: October 27, 1969

Nikon

Kodak

Kodak Professional Division

Our thanks to our corporate sponsors who, through their commitment to excellence in the visual arts, have helped make this project possible. In all aspects of the creation of this book we have endeavored to use the finest materials and avail ourselves of state-of-the-art services. The products and services of the companies who have participated in the making of *From the Sea* are second to none. And once again, our warmest thanks and appreciation to the many fine men and women of America's Armed Forces, some of whom are pictured on this page.